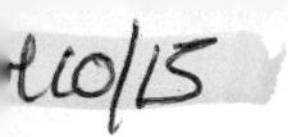

LENIN AND REVOLUTIONARY RUSSIA

QUESTIONS AND ANALYSIS IN HISTORY

Edited by Stephen J. Lee, Sean Lang and Jocelyn Hunt

Other titles in this series:

Modern History

Imperial Germany, 1871–1918
Stephen J. Lee

The Weimar Republic
Stephen J. Lee

Hitler and Nazi Germany
Stephen J. Lee

The Spanish Civil War
Andrew Forrest

The Cold War
Bradley Lightbody

Stalin and the Soviet Union
Stephen J. Lee

Parliamentary Reform, 1785–1928
Sean Lang

British Foreign and Imperial Policy, 1865–1919
Graham D. Goodlad

The French Revolution
Jocelyn Hunt

The First World War
Ian C. Cawood and David McKinnon-Bell

Anglo-Irish Relations, 1798–1922
Nick Pelling

Churchill
Samantha Heywood

Mussolini and Fascism
Patricia Knight

Early Modern History

The English Wars and Republic, 1636–1660
Graham E. Seel

The Renaissance
Jocelyn Hunt

Tudor Government
T. A. Morris

Spain, 1474–1598
Jocelyn Hunt

The Early Stuart Kings, 1603–1642
Graham E. Seel and David L. Smith

Redcar & Cleveland College
00055373

First published 2003
by Routledge
2 Park Square, Milton Park, Abingdon, Oxon OX14 4RN

Simultaneously published in the USA and Canada
by Routledge
270 Madison Avenue, New York, NY 10016

Reprinted 2005
Transferred to Digital Printing 2006

Routledge is an imprint of the Taylor & Francis Group, an informa business

Typeset in Akzidenz Grotesk and Perpetua by
Keystroke, Jacaranda Lodge, Wolverhampton
Printed and bound in Great Britain by
Biddles Ltd, King's Lynn, Norfolk

British Library Cataloguing in Publication Data
A catalogue record for this book is available from the British Library

Library of Congress Cataloguing in Publication Data
Lee, Stephen J., 1945–
Lenin and revolutionary Russia / Stephen J. Lee.
p. cm.—(Questions and analysis in history)
Includes bibliographical references and index.
1. Russia—Politics and government—1894–1917. 2. Soviet Union—Politics and government—1917–1936. 3. Russian Communism (bolsheviks)—History. 4. Communism—Soviet Union—History. 5. Lenin, Vladimir Ilych, 1870–1924. I. Title. II. Series.

DK246.L427 2003
320.947′09′041—dc21 2003045912

ISBN 10: 0–415–28717–0 (hbk)
ISBN 10: 0–415–28718–9 (pbk)
ISBN 13: 978–0–415–28717–3 (hbk)
ISBN 13: 978–0–415–28718–0 (pbk)

For Charlotte

CONTENTS

INTRODUCTION

The *Questions and Analysis* series is based on the belief that the student actively benefits from explicit interpretation of key issues and help with source-based technique. Each volume therefore separates narrative from analysis and sources; it follows an overall structure of Background Narrative, Analyses, and Sources with questions and worked answers.

This volume, *Lenin and Revolutionary Russia*, is the first in the series to add another dimension. Sixth-form and university courses have given increasing importance to historical debates, requiring proficiency in historiography as well as history. The revised format takes this development into account.

Chapter 1, therefore, provides some general explanations of why historians differ in their interpretation of key historical issues. The subsequent chapters follow a common pattern. The Background is confined to essential introductory perspectives or narrative. Analysis (1) focuses on a key historical issue (as in previous volumes), while Analysis (2) now examines the historiographical dimensions of the same issue, considering the extent of and reasons for changes of emphasis. In examination terms, Analysis (1) is in line with the requirements of AS and Analysis (2) with A2. They are, however, interlinked: Analysis (1) provides the material the student needs to know before being able to deal with A2 perspectives, while Analysis (2) gives the AS student a view of the next logical development in interpretation – and an insight into the implications of A2. The Sources also vary in their approach. The main principle is that the first set of Sources and Questions in each chapter is aimed at developing AS skills; the style of Sources and Questions varies to provide an overlap with each of the examining boards. The second set of Sources, relating to A2, follows the pattern broadly associated with one board, which offers the topic in its specifications. Where (as in Chapters 2 and 8) there is only one set of Sources, the subject matter is largely historiographical and therefore related to A2.

This book also aims to interest students in higher education, who might find a background to history and historiography helpful for their chosen topic. The Sources and Questions offer a variety of approaches and techniques that are likely to provide at least a starting point for further analysis. The series as a whole has kept in mind the interest of an increasingly sophisticated general reader, perhaps coming to a particular topic as a result of television, which emphasises new ideas in history.

The subject of this volume could not be more controversial. Lenin's reputation has been subject to a wider range of interpretations than that of any other major historical figure. He was a force for fundamental good – or evil. He was crucial for the growth of revolution in Russia – or peripheral to it. He was a liberator – or an autocrat. He based his actions on ideas – or his ideas followed his actions. He was consistent – or inconsistent. He led the masses – or followed them. His plans came to fruition under Stalin – or were betrayed by Stalin. And finally, the Soviet regime collapsed in spite of his influence – or because of it.

It is hoped that the student or general reader will want to contribute to the debate in these chapters. Such a range of ideas is bound to stimulate more. Provided that they can be substantiated, they are all valid – and they all count. This is what makes history so creative.

CHRONOLOGY

Russia used the Julian calendar under Tsariam, so in 1917 the two revolutions may be termed February and October (Julian) or March and November (Gregorian). The Julian calendar is used for all dates in this book up to 1918: The Bolsheviks adopted the Gregorian calendar in February 1918.

1883 Formation of the Emancipation of Labour (a Marxist group) by Plekhanov.
1895 Formation of the Fighting Union for the Liberation of the Working Class by Lenin.
1898 Publication of Lenin's *Tasks of the Russian Social Democrats*. Formation of Russian Social Democratic Labour Party (RSDLP) from the Emancipation of Labour and the Fighting Union for the Liberation of the Working Class.
1899 Publication of Lenin's *The Development of Capitalism in Russia*.
1900 Formation of the Socialist Revolutionary Party from various populist groups. Foundation of the RSDLP paper *Iskra*.
1902 Publication of Lenin's *What Is to Be Done?*
1903 Publication of Lenin's *To the Rural Poor*. Second Congress of RSDLP in Brussels and London, resulting in split between Lenin and Martov – Bolsheviks and Mensheviks (July–August).
1904 Publication of Lenin's *One Step Forward, Two Steps Back* and Martov's *Struggle with the State of Siege in the RSDLP*. Outbreak of Russo-Japanese War.
1905 Publication of Lenin's *Two Tactics of Social Democracy in the Democratic Revolution*. Bloody Sunday and the beginning of the 1905 Revolution (January). Formation of Petrograd Soviet. Russia's defeat in Russo-Japanese War. October: Tsar's October Manifesto.
1906 Fundamental Laws promulgated. First Duma convened.

1907 Second Duma convened (February). New Electoral Law (June). Third Duma convened (November).
1912 Strikes in the Lena goldfields. Fourth Duma convened (November).
1914 General strikes in Baku and St Petersburg. Outbreak of war against Germany and Austria-Hungary. St Petersburg renamed Petrograd.
1915 Strike action throughout European Russia. Command of the Russian forces assumed by Nicholas II. Zimmerwald Conference of revolutionary parties (August).
1916 Publication of Lenin's *Imperialism: The Highest Stage of Capitalism.* Conference of revolutionary parties in Kienthal (April). Major strikes in Petrograd (October). Assassination of Rasputin (December).
1917 Publication of Lenin's *The State and Revolution.* Overthrow of Tsarist regime and formation of Petrograd Soviet and Provisional Government under Lvov (February). Return of Lenin to Russia. Publication of *April Theses.* Failure of attempt to overthrow Provisional Government (July). Lenin in hiding in Finland. Resignation of Lvov and replacement as head of the Provisional Government by Kerensky. Attempted coup by General Kornilov. Bolshevik aid enlisted by Kerensky to overcome Kornilov (August–September). Trotsky elected President of Petrograd Soviet. Bolshevik majorities in Petrograd and Moscow soviets. Formation of Revolutionary Military Committee (September–October). Bolshevik Revolution and overthrow of the Provisional Government. Meeting of All-Russian Congress of Soviets (October). Elections for Constituent Assembly. Establishment of Cheka.
1918 Dissolution of Constituent Assembly by Lenin (January). Protest by Socialist Revolutionaries and Mensheviks. Formation of Komuch programme. End of war between Germany and Russia by Treaty of Brest-Litovsk (March). Beginning of the Russian Civil War. Socialist Revolutionary governments established (e.g. Ufa Directorate) in defiance of Bolsheviks. White coups and campaigns. Constitution of the RSFSR (July). Killing of Tsar and family by Bolsheviks at Ekaterinberg. Foreign intervention in support of the Whites. Introduction of War Communism.
1919 Defeat of White campaigns under Kolchak, Yudenitch, Deniken and Wrangel. Withdrawal of foreign troops.
1920 War between Soviet Russia and Poland (ended 1921). Resistance to Bolshevik regime by peasant armies.
1921 Kronstadt uprising (March). End of War Communism and introduction of New Economic Policy (NEP).
1922 Activities of the Cheka suspended.
1923 Codicil added to Lenin's Testament (January).
1924 Death of Lenin (21 January).
1924–9 The interregnum and struggle between Stalin and Trotsky.

1929–53 Stalin in power.

1953–64 Khrushchev in power. Destalinisation campaign from 1956 onwards.

1964–82 Brezhnev in power.

1985–91 Gorbachev in power. Policies of *glasnost* and *perestroika*.

1991 End of the Soviet Union (December).

1

WHY DO HISTORICAL INTERPRETATIONS DIFFER?

The study of history has two dimensions, which are revealed by the Latin and Greek words that form the roots of the term itself. One is the record or account of the past. The other is the explanation given to the story. It is a method of enquiry that seeks answers to questions and is derived from the Greek roots *histor* (learned, wise man) and *oida* (the verb to know). The most obvious changes occur in the *methods of enquiry*, although these do eventually affect the shape of the account or story.

CHANGES IN THE STYLES OF HISTORY

The main reason for this change is the constant evolution of history as an academic discipline. One of the earlier uses of history was as a means of interpreting human behaviour and human society. This would, in turn, be subject to broader laws, which the main purpose of history was to illustrate and exemplify. In the Middle Ages, for example, history showed the development of mankind during the temporal phase of its progression to eternity. What really mattered was the religious concept of salvation, which transcended human achievement but could be earned by following some of the lessons from the past while avoiding others. In this sense history served a higher purpose and had no separate justification; as a result, it tended to be prescriptive and moralising. Although religion gradually declined as a key influence on historical interpretation, it was replaced by other 'systems'. One is particularly relevant to this book: the Marxist approach, which emerged during the nineteenth century and was given official political sanction and force after the Bolshevik Revolution. The Marxist approach was given an official slant – and sanction – by the Soviet regime and it is this particular version of retrospective determinism that provides the starting point for each of the following chapters.

Other forms of history have largely escaped deterministic influences, focusing on criteria related to the subject itself, rather than on broader 'world views' imposed from outside. Even here, however, there have been major changes over the past 150 years. These relate largely to academic concepts of what comprises history. A major connection with the nineteenth century can be seen in what Herbert Butterfield referred to as 'Whig' history. This is seen as a broad sweep of historical development, in which there are prominent landmarks and in which the overall trend is progressive. The key influence here is the nineteenth-century historian and politician Thomas Babington Macaulay (1800–59), whose main focus was the development of the British political system since the Glorious Revolution of 1689. It is still possible to see elements of 'Whig' history, especially where there are value judgements, either open or implied, within a substantial timescale. It is not, however, a description that historians would particularly welcome, since Butterfield used it as a criticism.

The exact opposite was the emergence of what has sometimes been called 'Tory' history. This is normally associated with the methods used by Sir Lewis Namier (1888–1960), based on more detailed and meticulous examination of much shorter periods, without any intrusion of moral judgement. 'Namierisation' has provided the inspiration for a great deal of modern historical research, although it has been criticised for being largely unconcerned about broader perspectives. A third important development was the 'Annales' school of Marc Bloch (1886–1944) and Lucien Febvre (1878–1956). Their approach was to combine a broad sweep with detailed analysis, the latter covering economic, social and cultural – as well as political – history.

All this had considerable implications for the way in which history developed as a discipline during the twentieth century. At first the emphasis within the subject had been very much on *political* history, with the study of power and the formulation and impact of the policy of groups and key individuals. A second area had been *economic* history, concerned more with infrastructures than with policies and frequently studied separately from political history. A major development, however, was the expansion of *social* history. Although this had long been present, it had been the poor relation of political and economic history. Under the influence of the Annales approach, however, it produced a rich variety of historical studies that later included local, gender and ethnic issues. As a result of this diversity, history as a discipline has had to find a new centre of gravity. Although political history has tended to remain the predominant genre, its scope has widened in response to such studies.

All of these developments are apparent in the evolution of works of Western historians on the Soviet Union, especially on the Lenin and Stalin periods. Early assessments tended to be based firmly on the development of power structures by individuals and the use of those structures for certain specific objectives. They were, in other words, strongly political; economic and social developments were examined for the impact of the policies of those in control upon those who were being controlled. The same principle applied whether the controlling force was a revolutionary leader establishing a new movement (Lenin to 1917) or an established regime that was redesigning and restructuring (Lenin 1918–24 and Stalin 1929–53). Power came from above and the effects were received from below.

The changing emphasis of history as a discipline has had a huge impact on how this power is now seen. Not only is it imposed from above on those below; it can also be exercised from below as a collective force that pulls into line those above. This approach is certainly relevant to Russian history, especially to the way in which the Bolsheviks are seen in relation to the proletariat and peasantry. Detailed research in the field of social history has established the importance of small-scale organisations and radicalism among large sections of the population. Far from being inert and conservative, the peasantry were politically conscious; and the urban workers were certainly not a leaderless rabble awaiting organisation from above.

The more complete the picture of the lower levels of society, the more likely it was that the perspective would change on the types of power and leadership traditionally considered the crucial factors. Social history has therefore redefined the scope of political and economic history qualitatively by drawing attention to the quantitative influence of humanity.

There is no reason to suppose that history as an academic discipline will not continue to change its shape and emphasis, bringing further reinterpretation to Russia and other areas in the future. There are three possible overall trends that could perhaps be given a cosmic metaphor. One is that history will expand ever outwards – diversifying and subdividing into a variety of new disciplines that are no longer considered to be formally connected to each other; history will simply disintegrate. Another is that history will retain some form of gravitational pull and that whatever changes of structure take place in the future, the various components will hold together. Or there may be a combination of the two: apparent disintegration followed by reintegration. Much will depend on the skill with which detailed and specialised studies can be synthesised within a more general structure. In this sense general histories will be of vital importance to ensure that history retains a force of gravity amid widespread changes.

INFLUENCES BEHIND RECENT CHANGES

These changes are driven and accelerated by historical research, for four main reasons. First, research keeps the discipline moving forward by introducing new material that prevents reassessment from being merely recycling. The *discovery* of new sources is a crucial factor here. This may be fortuitous or the result of a careful and painstaking search. There is often a political reason – such as the introduction of *glasnost* in 1987 and the collapse of the Soviet Union at the end of 1991; both of these led to a gradual opening of documentary archives that had previously been kept secret by the Stalinist regime and its successors. New documents have, for example, provided fresh insights into Lenin's exercise of power and the extent to which his polices were opportunist.

Second, research accelerates the *speed* at which history moves. This is because research is an expectation within the higher academic levels: it has become a criterion for higher academic qualification. Since research requires originality of approach, depth of study and soundness of method, it is bound to contribute massively to the diversity of historical interpretation as well as historical detail. In this way, universities have created an environment that has to be sustained by continuous growth and change.

Third, research can exert more general influences on historical writing, establishing *styles* of investigation that can transfer from one country to another. An example is the spread of a particular form of analysis on Germany, developed in the 1960s and 1970s, to Russia in the 1980s and 1990s. The theory of 'structured chaos', originally used as a means of examining the Nazi regime by Fischer, Bracher, Broszat, Hildebrand and Kershaw, has now been applied to Lenin and Stalin by Arch Getty, Ward, Fitzpatrick and Swain. When applied in conjunction with 'pressures from below' this 'structured chaos' can be given further variations and generate a wide range of sub-debates.

Fourth, research generates the *publication* of academic monographs that, in turn, promote the spread of more general works. These are of several types. They may be symposia, or a selection of recent views for more accessible comparison. Alternatively, they may be a general synthesis drawn up by one of the historians engaged in research in the area – with the intention of making sense of complex issues to a wider public. These, in turn, inspire non-research-based syntheses, often for use in schools, colleges and further education, as textbooks. A change to an examination system or syllabus can further establish a link between the school, college and university sectors, thus generating further writing at a more general level.

Changes in political systems can also alter historical perspectives. This can happen in several ways. It may be direct or indirect, obvious or subtle. The most direct changes in interpretation occur when a regime that is in control of its historiography dictates a change in its history. The best example is the Soviet Union. After the death of Lenin, Stalin ordered that he should be written more firmly into the Russian Revolution as Lenin's main comrade. Trotsky, by contrast, was to be classed a traitor. When Khrushchev replaced Stalin, the latter was written out of Soviet history altogether, while Trotsky remained a villain. Further changes occurred with the liberalisation of the Soviet system under Gorbachev's *glasnost*. It has to be said, however, that Soviet versions of Lenin have remained remarkably consistent, even though they have changed in their interpretations of other Communist leaders. This reflects the special status accorded to Lenin as the founder of the regime.

Changes of regime in Russia have also affected Western interpretations. Khrushchev's destalinisation campaign from 1956 provided further evidence of the terror inflicted under his rule, which, naturally enough, intensified the hostility of Western historians to him. This also affected Lenin, as many historians looked back from the Stalinist era into what they saw as its Leninist roots. Lenin came increasingly to be seen as the forerunner of Stalin. Both were effective leaders, but were fundamentally ruthless. The collapse of the Soviet Union in 1991 raised a major question. If the Soviet Union had survived in war only to die in peace, then what sort of regime had controlled it throughout its existance? This led to more negative perspectives on Stalin: he must have been less effective than had previously been maintained. In turn, there was some reassessment of the role played by Lenin: his part, too, was toned down, although in different ways.

Historians see their task as creative as well as analytical. There is a longstanding debate as to whether history is an art or a science. It is both, since it combines scrupulous concern for evidence with creative interpretation, although not to such a degree that distortion occurs. Inevitably, therefore, historians differ in their approaches to particular topics and often cultivate these differences in articles, journals, books, lectures and televised debates.

Questions

1. 'History is made by historians.' Is this true?
2. Do historians 'liberate' or 'colonise' the past?
3. Are historians the 'product of the society in which they live'?
4. 'Who can tell what is going to happen yesterday?' Comment on this view.

2

OVERVIEW: THE BOLSHEVIK PARTY AND REGIME, 1903–24

BACKGROUND

The purpose of the first Analysis of this chapter is to provide a straightforward overall perspective of the origins of the Bolsheviks, their development to 1917, their role in the revolutions of 1917, their survival from 1918 and their transformation of Russia to 1924. The second Analysis provides an introduction to several different historical approaches to Lenin and the Bolsheviks, showing how controversial the topic has become.

The four Sources provided have a general theme and focus on the period as a whole. Since their scope is the overall perspective of the period they are, by definition, secondary sources. They have all been written since the events as retrospective interpretations of them.

ANALYSIS (1): HOW DID THE BOLSHEVIKS DEVELOP AS A REVOLUTIONARY PARTY BETWEEN 1903 AND 1917 AND AS A REGIME BETWEEN 1918 AND 1924?

1898–1903

The Bolsheviks originated as part of a broader Marxist political party, set up by Lenin, Martov and Plekhanov in 1898. Known as the Russian Social Democratic Labour Party (RSDLP), this united a number of smaller

Marxist radical groups that had, since the early 1880s, been emerging in Russia as an alternative form of radicalism to the essentially peasant-based populist movement. The RSDLP promoted the Marxist vision of the overthrow of capitalism, the creation of the 'dictatorship of the proletariat' and the eventual achievement of the 'classless society'; these ideas were publicised through *Iskra* (*The Spark*). From the start, however, Lenin pressed for a distinctive and active strategy, which he outlined in his pamphlet *What Is to Be Done?* (1902). By the time of the Second Congress of the RSDLP in 1903 these had been formalised into a disciplined and conspiratorial party structure and an acceleration of the process of revolutionary change. The moderate tendency within the RSDLP, led by Martov, favoured a more open, democratic and evolutionary role for Russian Marxism.

1905–March 1917

At first the Bolshevik–Menshevik breach was considered temporary and efforts were made to reunite the two factions as Social Democrats. But the divisions widened, partly because of Lenin's insistence on his particular approach. The two blocs became separate political parties. The Mensheviks were willing to collaborate with any opposition to the Tsarist regime, as they showed during the 1905 Revolution, for which Lenin accused them of being 'opportunists' who were betraying the Marxist cause. The Bolshevik approach was to bring down the Tsarist regime and to proceed as quickly as possible to the dictatorship of the proletariat without, as the Mensheviks were willing to concede, a prolonged period of co-operation with the bourgeoisie within a liberal democracy.

By 1914 both the Bolsheviks and the Mensheviks claimed that they had the more appropriate strategy to overcome Tsarist autocracy. It soon became clear, however, that the First World War would be a decisive factor, which is why they both welcomed it. Lenin produced the more forceful theory in his *Imperialism: The Highest Stage of Capitalism*. He argued strongly that the foreign war should be 'converted into a civil war'. In practical terms, however, the role of the Bolsheviks was limited. Lenin remained in exile in Geneva until 1917 and, although there was some Bolshevik activism in the trenches and factories, this was by no means decisive. The Mensheviks, on the other hand, were prepared to collaborate with the Progressive Bloc of moderate middle-class parties in the Duma, or state assembly, and with the populists or Socialist Revolutionaries. When the Tsarist regime reached a political crisis at the end of 1916 the Bolsheviks were the only major group not to be substantially connected with its overthrow. The Mensheviks and Socialist Revolutionaries became involved in the spontaneous uprising in February/ March 1917 and comprised a substantial proportion of delegates in the newly formed Petrograd Soviet. They also collaborated with the Provisional Government, set up by the Duma to replace the Tsar. The Bolsheviks were uninvolved in either. This could be seen as the lowest point of their influence throughout the period 1903–24.

March–October 1917

This changed with remarkable speed and at no other time did Lenin respond so rapidly to the situation. Within weeks he had arranged with the German government safe passage from Switzerland to the Baltic, from where he was able to return to Russia, and to issue, in the form of the *April Theses*, a programme designed to appeal to all parts of the proletariat and peasantry. The Bolsheviks became involved in an abortive coup in July, from which Lenin deduced the importance of precise timing for any future attempt. Between July and October/November the fortunes of the Bolsheviks rose as those of the Provisional Government fell. The latter was still giving priority to winning the war against Germany, Austria-Hungary and Turkey, even though this meant postponing key undertakings such as the calling of a constituent assembly and reforms over land and industry. As a result, substantial popular support swung behind the Bolsheviks, who promised to deliver these changes immediately. From August onwards the Provisional Government experienced a series of crises that deflected it from the firm line it had previously tried to take against the Bolsheviks; it even had to arm the Bolsheviks in a desperate move to put down a military coup by General Kornilov. By the beginning of October the transformation was complete: the Provisional Government had lost most of its earlier support, while the Bolsheviks had achieved a majority in the Petrograd Soviet, to which Trotsky was elected President. From this Lenin deduced that the time was right for a second revolution, which was carried out on 24/25 October (6/7 November in the Gregorian calendar) by the Revolutionary Military Committee of the Duma, or the Red Guard. The Provisional Government, deprived of almost all of its defences, collapsed overnight.

1918–24

Seizing power was one thing, maintaining it quite another, as between 1918 and 1921 the Bolsheviks had to fight to keep and extend their authority against a variety of groups who were determined to remove them. The Mensheviks and Socialist Revolutionaries objected forcefully to Lenin's decision to close the Constituent Assembly after it had produced a minority for the Bolsheviks, and proceeded to set up their own governments to the east of the area under Bolshevik control. Events were, however, overtaken by the involvement of the Whites, or counter-revolutionaries, who advanced on the Bolshevik heartland from all directions. Having made peace with Germany at Brest-Litovsk in March 1918, the Bolsheviks were able to focus all their resources on winning the Civil War. This had been largely accomplished by 1921, although the Bolsheviks still had the difficult task of dealing with extensive revolts from the peasantry.

Organising the Bolshevik state for victory involved major political changes as Russia came under authoritarian rule. The brief experiment with such Western-style institutions as the Constituent Assembly was replaced by a one-party state that operated through a hierarchy of soviets, all under Bolshevik control. The Communist Party Central Committee also dominated all the executive organs of the state, including the Central Executive Committee and Politburo. All other parties and any opposition were systematically eliminated by the Cheka, the police force introduced to co-ordinate a period of terror between 1918 and 1921. By the time that the Civil War had ended, Bolshevik Russia (by then renamed Soviet Russia) had become a monolithic dictatorship.

There was also every intention to transform the economy, but this proved more difficult in the circumstances of privation produced by the Civil War. Initial changes, from the end of 1917 until the beginning of 1918, included the nationalisation only of armaments works, banks and foreign trade. Between 1918 and 1921, however, Lenin resorted to the policy of War Communism as a means of imposing state control over all industry while simultaneously requisitioning grain from the peasantry to feed workers in the cities and soldiers in the Red Army. This, however, generated enormous opposition, in effect prolonging the Civil War through a series of peasant uprisings and bringing the Bolshevik regime close to collapse. As a result, Lenin was forced into a more pragmatic line based on concessions. The New Economic Policy, introduced in 1921, therefore ended requisitioning, denationalised most industries and allowed for a degree of 'state capitalism'. The Bolsheviks could afford to backtrack on the economy because they had total political control. There were, however, many different views over which direction the economy should take in the future.

Conclusion

Between 1903 and 1924, therefore, Bolshevism underwent a gradual transformation. It had started as strategy, or 'tendency', within a broader Marxist movement. Under Lenin's forceful insistence, the tendency itself became a party, which was committed to revolution in the short rather than long term. This met with very mixed success between 1905 and February/March 1917, coming into its own mainly from April 1917. From this stage it capitalised on the loss of revolutionary impetus of the other parties and filled the gap that they had left. Success in October was so sudden that it could have been premature. The Bolsheviks had an enormous struggle to establish a permanent government and the timescale involved in converting Bolshevism from a party into a regime was much shorter than had been the case in the conversion of a strategy into a party.

Questions

1. Why did Marxism divide in Russia – and with what results?
2. Did a 'revolutionary party' become a 'revolutionary dictatorship'?

ANALYSIS (2): HOW HAVE INTERPRETATIONS DIFFERED OVER THE ORIGINS AND SURVIVAL OF THE BOLSHEVIK PARTY AND REGIME BETWEEN 1903 AND 1924?

Considering its immediate and long-term effects, the creation of the Bolshevik regime in Russia was arguably the most important event of the first half of the twentieth century. It is therefore hardly surprising that there should have been a number of widely differing interpretations of the reasons for this phenomenon. Three main approaches can be identified, although each has its own range of variations.

The official 'Soviet' view

The first is the official line provided by the government of the Soviet Union. This is available in publications such as *A Short History of the Communist Party of the Soviet Union,*[1] prepared by a committee of historians acting under political directives. Although the sections on Stalin have been extensively changed, those on Lenin have remained remarkably consistent, claiming that the founder of the Communist regime always acted strictly in the interests of the Marxist ideology and the

Russian working people. The achievements of the Bolsheviks are clearly mapped out, as are the obstacles presented by their enemies. It is very much a story of the triumph of right over wrong – within the simplified parameters set by a totalitarian regime. There are no contradictions or subtleties of argument; no reservations or alternatives; no unresolved inner tensions. Everything is in red and white. Although the result makes for bad analytical history (and tedious reading), it is useful as an example of polemicism and propaganda. It also provides structures to be criticised by alternative approaches.

The basis of the official Soviet view is as follows. By the late nineteenth century the vast majority of the Russian people were being exploited by traditional Russian feudalism and by a newly emergent entrepreneurial capitalist class. The latter brought Russia into the scope of the Marxist theories that 'The history of all hitherto existing society is the history of class conflict' and that the industrial proletariat would eventually emerge triumphant over those classes that had previously exploited it. Russia did not fit the Marxist specifications precisely because its industrial proletariat was much smaller than the rural peasantry. Nevertheless, the formation of the Russian Social Democratic Labour Party in 1898 was a strong move in that direction. One of its co-founders, Lenin, realised that Marxism would have to be adapted to Russian conditions if it were to embrace the peasantry as well. Unfortunately, there were certain individuals within the RSDLP who interpreted Marxism as requiring a long period of collaboration with the middle class, or bourgeoisie, before any far-reaching social change could be established, which in turn questioned the need for a revolution at all. At the Second RSDLP Congress in 1903, Lenin refuted these arguments of Martov and established the Bolsheviks' revolutionary credentials against the collaborationism of the Mensheviks.

The 1905 Revolution was a spontaneous attempt by the Russian working class to throw off Tsarist autocracy, but was betrayed by the Mensheviks' willingness to come to terms with the regime. The Bolsheviks, by contrast, learned from the failure of the revolution the need for more effective organisation. Between 1905 and 1914 they tried to reunite the Marxist groups within Russia but came to realise that the Mensheviks were determined to sell out to the middle class in the impossible hope of reforming the Tsarist regime. It was quite clear, therefore, that the Bolsheviks were the only party truly representing Marxist principles. By 1914 the industrial proletariat were moving behind the Bolsheviks and were becoming increasingly involved in industrial action. The workers were clearly convinced by Lenin's interpretation of Marxist revolution.

The First World War then intervened. It was not sought by the Bolsheviks but was used by them as a weapon to achieve the revolution: the 'imperialist' war was turned into a 'civil' war to eliminate 'capitalist exploitation'. Bolshevik encouragement and organisation lay behind the strikes of 1915 and 1916 and did much to promote the uprising of February 1917 that swept away the Tsarist regime. Unfortunately, that victory was perverted by the Mensheviks and Socialist Revolutionaries, who collaborated with the Provisional Government. This was a bourgeois–liberal regime that had no intention of considering the real interests of the industrial proletariat or the peasantry. On his return from exile in April 1917 Lenin therefore prepared to take the revolution through into a second, democratic phase. This was accomplished in October, when the Bolsheviks seized power from the Provisional Government.

From the start the new regime was confronted by opposition from reactionary and counter-revolutionary elements, known as the Whites, who were assisted by the Mensheviks and the majority of the Socialist Revolutionaries. The Bolsheviks therefore organised to defend their new state and, in winning the Civil War between 1918 and 1921, gradually liberated the whole of Russia to Communism. A more advanced and democratic system was set up, based on a network of soviets under the overall supervision of the Communist Party of the Soviet Union (CPSU) and a new federal constitution was introduced for Russia in 1918. After a short period of hardship, a 'mixed' economic system was permitted until the country had developed sufficiently to move towards full socialism.

By 1924, therefore, the Bolsheviks had succeeded in their objectives because they alone had the support of the population and the organisation to overcome minority opposition to it. Through Lenin's guidance and leadership, they alone showed the correctness of the Marxist prediction that the proletariat would eventually triumph.

Various Western approaches

Western historians have differing interpretations of Lenin and the Bolsheviks. These range from the openly favourable to the obviously hostile.

There might be two reasons for a favourable approach. One relates to a time factor. Many of the earliest studies of Lenin and the Russian Revolution were compiled by Western observers – often journalists – who visited Russia and came into direct contact with Lenin and other Bolshevik leaders. They were therefore relying primarily on personal impressions and documents that would have been made available to them by a regime struggling for survival against apparently huge odds.

They would also have influenced, and been influenced by, the swing of substantial sectors of Western public opinion against the forces of counter-revolution in the latter stage of the Civil War. Examples include Max Eastman, an American journalist and historian who published *Marx, Lenin and the Science of Revolution* in 1926.[2] A second reason is more fundamental. As an 'open society', the West contained a much wider spectrum of political sympathies than would have existed in a monolithic state like the Soviet Union. This meant that there were bound to be some pro-Marxist historians in Western Europe. One was Christopher Hill, a university academic historian, whose *Lenin and the Russian Revolution* (published in 1947) was unusually sympathetic to Lenin as both a revolutionary and a statesman.[3] Another was John Rees, who was also involved in political activity as a leading member of Britain's Socialist Workers' Party.[4]

Lenin has also invoked hostility from the West. The main catalyst for this was probably the freezing climate of the Cold War, especially during the late 1940s and 1950s. Stalin and his system were seen as major threats to democracy and their roots were traced back to Lenin. In 1953 the American political scientist Merle Fainsod,[5] emphasised the military nature of the Bolshevik seizure of power, a theme that became fundamental to a wave of interpretation that the October Revolution took power *from* the people, not *for* them. The Cold War thawed for a while in the late 1950s when the new Soviet ruler, Khrushchev, chose to reveal to the world the full extent of the brutality of Stalin's regime up to 1953. This theme was taken up by historians like Robert Conquest, who provided unprecedented detail about the horrors of Stalinism – and then went on to make the link with the Bolsheviks in a brief biography, *Lenin*.[6]

Between these two wings were to be found other historians who adopt a more cautious approach, trying where possible to avoid both favourable and hostile comments on Lenin. Almost without exception, however, these credited Lenin as the progenitor of Bolshevism and the architect of Bolshevik success in 1917. In many ways they overlapped the views of the more radical trends, only with the judgements deleted.

Western historians sympathetic to Lenin have emphasised the importance of his ideas and strategies in making a genuine adjustment to Marxist ideology to suit Russian conditions. This involved a degree of ruthlessness and conspiracy, but Lenin considered that there was no other way. Those more critical of Lenin believed that the Bolsheviks did not so much adapt Marxist *revolutionary* theory to Russia's economic conditions as distort Marxist *economic* theory to Russia's revolutionary traditions. Lenin's approach to revolutionary organisation was conspiratorial and authoritarian, very much in line with earlier radicalism in Russia. As a result there was a different perception of Bolsheviks in relation to the Mensheviks. Either they were seen as trying to compensate for the weakness of the Mensheviks by setting up a tighter party structure, or they were deliberately undermining the Menshevik strategy of broad collaboration with all anti-Tsarist groups. Either way, the Bolsheviks operated as a disciplined and professional revolutionary group, gradually extending their control over workers' organisations in the industrial areas and using propaganda and subversion to try to create the right environment for a seizure of power.

The First World War provided the Bolsheviks with the opportunity to destabilise the regime, especially through agitation in the army and among the industrial workforce. No Western historian has seriously denied that the Bolsheviks played comparatively little part in the February Revolution, which was largely a spontaneous uprising. But there have been divergent views over what happened next. Some see Lenin as fulfilling the wishes and needs of the population, sight of which had been lost by the other revolutionary groups and the Provisional Government. Others, however, see Lenin's success as pure opportunism; ever the flexible pragmatist, Lenin used the difficulties faced by the Provisional Government to strengthen the position of the Bolsheviks and to prepare for an armed coup. This was achieved by conspiratorial methods, and without popular support, in October. The Bolshevik coup succeeded because of the weakness of the party's opponents and the strength of its own organisation and leadership.

On one thing most Western historians agreed, until recently. The coup of October 1917 became a real revolution between 1918 and 1924 as the Bolsheviks transformed the whole structure of Russia. The agent of this transformation was the Civil War, as the Bolsheviks mobilised the population against the Whites. They also used the conflict to revolutionise the political structure through the introduction of a new system based on the CPSU and the soviets. This, in turn, was reinforced by the calculated used of terror in the form of the Cheka. The one area where revolution could not be effectively applied was the economy. After the failure of the initial radical approach – War Communism – pragmatism dictated a temporary retreat into the New Economic Policy (NEP). The difference in interpretation comes with the judgement that goes with all this. Was the whole process due to a revolution making a legitimate struggle for survival against counter-revolution? Or was it a more ruthless extension of the power seized in October 1917?

Revisionist approaches

Revisionism involves a fundamental reassessment of earlier views that had been widely accepted. This may take several forms. In the case of Lenin and the Bolsheviks there are two.

One took place in Russia before and after the collapse of the Soviet Union. The main target of Soviet revisionism was Stalin, who, for almost twenty years after 1960, was written out of Soviet history altogether. Although, for a while, the historical position of Lenin was as strong as ever, some tarnish began to show from the mid-1980s; it was at this time that a policy of greater 'openness' (*glasnost*) was promoted by Gorbachev and criticism of the Soviet regime began to touch even its venerated founder. It is true that Lenin was never demonised in the way that Stalin had been, but some of his methods were open to question and more emphasis was placed on the 'heroic' achievements of the Russian people than on the party and leadership that had made them possible.

At this point there is an overlap with a much more powerful current of revisionism – from the West. Here, too, Lenin and the Bolsheviks have been cut down to size. The underlying argument of historians such as Rabinowitch is that the Russian people were spontaneously revolutionary.[7] The workers were highly conscious politically, while large parts of the peasantry were instinctively radical. Detailed research has reversed former assumptions that the population, especially in the rural areas, needed to be stimulated into action and their power channelled by such organisations as the Bolsheviks. It now seems that the Bolsheviks were the ones who were pushed; there is clear evidence of this throughout the period 1903–17. The following summary is based primarily on Western revisionism, although there is some overlap with the Soviet variant.

The initial activities of the Social Democrats were considered to be inadequate by organisations representing both workers and the more radical peasants. Hence Russian Marxists found that they were being pushed into a more radical phase in 1903 by growing pressures from below. When Lenin opted for a more tightly structured organisation and an accelerated programme of revolution, he was trying to respond to these pressures and keep the initiative. In this respect, it could be argued, the Bolsheviks, more than the Mensheviks, were in tune with the activist trends within Russian labour at the time.

The First World War was not of any particular benefit to the Bolsheviks; nor did they manage to use it effectively against the regime. Lenin may have theorised about the use of war to generate revolution, but the process was in reality spontaneous. Neither the strikes that caused such disruption in 1915 and 1916 nor the mutinies and desertions within the Russian armed forces were stimulated by the Bolsheviks. The February Revolution, similarly, had nothing to do with Bolshevik propaganda or subversion. Indeed, it took Lenin by surprise and he had to hurry back from Switzerland to catch up with events in Russia. From April 1917 Bolshevik policy moved into line with popular demands, often at the expense of earlier Marxist ideology: for example, Lenin's promise of private ownership of the land by the peasantry was entirely new. As a result, the Bolsheviks were more genuinely popular in the second half of 1917 than either the Mensheviks or the Socialist Revolutionaries, who were compromised by their relationship with the Provisional Government. Thus the Bolshevik Revolution was not a coup organised with ruthless efficiency against the wishes of the majority of the population, but a genuine revolution in which the Bolsheviks were swept along by a popular tide.

This new perspective on the Bolshevik Revolution has also given rise to a reassessment of the nature of the Bolshevik state from 1918 to 1924. The previous assumption was that the coup of October was followed by the revolution of 1918–24. Revisionist interpretation reverses this. The revolution of October gave way quickly to a period of reaction as Lenin and the Bolsheviks sought to close down the revolution. The main reason for this was their fear of other revolutionary strands, especially the Mensheviks and the Socialist Revolutionaries. The latter challenged the Bolshevik regime from several areas in Russia early in 1918. This meant that the Civil War was as much about eradicating alternative versions of revolution as it was about preventing counter-revolution from the Whites. To guarantee the permanence of their position, the Bolsheviks proceeded to establish a repressive regime with a monolithic political base enforced by ruthless terror. This might even be seen as the real counter-revolution of post-October.

Conclusion

These are three very different versions of a crucial phase of Russian history. Within them there are variations and sub-debates. Between them there are connecting links and huge gaps. The result is an endless variety of possible interpretations with, in skilful hands, some potential for creative synthesis.

Questions

1. Did Lenin and the Bolsheviks lead the masses or follow them?
2. Did Lenin 'plan' the revolution and the regime or did he 'discover' them?

SOURCES

PERSPECTIVES OF THE BOLSHEVIK REVOLUTION

Source A: Extract from A *Short History of the Communist Party of the Soviet Union*. This edition was published in Moscow in 1970. The work was prepared, under the guidance of the government of the USSR, by a committee of Soviet historians.

The Great October Socialist Revolution overthrew the anti-popular regime, smashed the obsolete state system . . . and created the Soviet socialist state.

Its distinctive feature is that it was accomplished by the working class in alliance with the poor peasantry. In the course of the revolution the workers and peasants set up soviets, which were the organs of the revolution. The soviets were not invented by any political party; they had been created by the masses themselves as far back as the first Russian revolution [in 1905] . . . The October Revolution turned them from revolutionary organs for mobilising and preparing the masses for an armed uprising into organs of the new workers' and peasants' power. Through them it was possible to draw the working masses into the administration of the state and the building of socialism . . .

It was a triumph of Marxism–Leninism and demonstrated the significance and role of the revolutionary Marxist Party. The working class and all other working people of Russia were led by the Bolshevik Party, which was guided by the revolutionary theory of Marxism-Leninism. The people saw that the Party was devoted to them and provided them with judicious leadership and recognised it as their leader.

Source B: Extracts from Merle Fainsod: *How Russia Is Ruled*, published in 1953. The author was Professor of Government at the University of Harvard, Massachusetts.

The Bolshevik Revolution was not a majoritarian movement. The last free elections in Russia, the elections to the Constituent Assembly which took place toward the end of 1917, clearly demonstrated that the Bolshevik voting strength in the country at large was not more than 25 per cent. But, as Lenin subsequently observed, the Bolsheviks did have 'an overwhelming preponderance of force at the decisive moment in the decisive points'. In the areas and units strategically important to the success of the insurrection – Petrograd, Moscow, the Baltic fleet, and the garrisons around Petrograd – Bolshevik ascendancy turned the scale. The enemies of Bolshevism were numerous, but they were also weak, poorly organized, divided and apathetic. The strategy of Lenin was calculated to emphasize their divisions, neutralize their opposition, and capitalize on their apathy. In 1902 in *What Is To Be Done?* Lenin had written, 'Give us an organization of revolutionaries, and we shall overturn the whole of Russia!' On November 7, 1917, the wish was fulfilled and the deed accomplished.

Source C: Extract from Edward Acton: *Rethinking the Russian Revolution*, published in 1990. At the time of publication the author was Professor of Modern European History at the University of East Anglia.

Revisionist work has exposed the shortcomings of [other historical interpretations]. It has traced the process which led to mass radicalization and underscored the autonomous and rational nature of the intervention by workers, soldiers and peasants. It has demonstrated the decisive impact of that intervention upon the fate of the Provisional Government and of the moderate socialists. It has brought out the strength the Bolshevik party derived from its responsiveness to popular aspirations and anxieties, from its relatively decentralized, tolerant and ideologically heterogeneous make-up, and from its readiness to defy as well as to follow Lenin. It has highlighted the plebeian composition of the party [and] the mass popularity it enjoyed in October 1917 . . . It has underlined the speed with which the party forfeited mass support in the aftermath of the revolution and shifted its power base from soviet democracy to administrative and military coercion. It has revealed the transformation that overcame the internal structure and composition of the party in the course of the Civil War.

Revisionist work points to a radical reinterpretation of the Russian revolution. Glasnost and the opening of long-closed archives promise to bring a fresh momentum to the effort to recover the real drama of 1917 from the myths that it inspired. But how far and how soon the labours of specialists will affect popular misconceptions remains to be seen. Old myths die hard.

Source D: Extract from *The Decline of Imperial Russia* by Hugh Seton-Watson, first published in 1952. The author was at the time of publication Professor of Modern History at the University of Oxford.

Once the doctrine of the conspiratorial vanguard of professional revolutionaries is accepted, everything else follows from it. Lenin's views on the relationship of the party to the Duma, to trade unions, to the agrarian problem and to the preparations for armed action are all a logical consequence of his view of the party. The Mensheviks denied the conspiratorial conception, and their views of the same four problems follow inevitably from the denial. Neither side can be proved absolutely right. The correctness of tactics depends on the situation in which they are to be applied. The political and economic evolution of Russia between 1906 and 1914 definitely supported the Menshevik view, but the situation in Russia in 1917 equally supported the Bolsheviks, theoretically as well as in practice. The Russian professional revolutionary is essentially the product of a society in which the nineteenth- or twentieth-century intellectual is driven to revolutionary action by the spectacle of his people living in the Middle Ages and unable to climb out of them . . . Russia was such a country in the days of People's Will, but she was ceasing to be in 1914. A large industrial working class, with considerable education, skill and class-consciousness, was becoming a real force. So was a bourgeois middle class. In such conditions the conspiratorial revolutionary was becoming an anachronism, and was so regarded by a growing number of Russian Marxists, both among workers and among intellectuals. To them Lenin, passionately defending the earlier type of organisation, seemed a utopian reactionary. Yet in 1917 Lenin's tactics were better suited to the facts than those of his opponents. Military defeat, economic chaos and famine in the cities had reduced Russia to a condition more primitive even than in the days of Alexander II. In this situation a group of revolutionary conspirators, clearly understanding what they wanted . . . were a match for any party modelled on the mass movements of Western Europe. Lenin in 1917 came into his own. Yet if history had not made him a present of chaos his talents might have been wasted in the frustration and intrigues of exile.

Questions

*1. How different are Sources A and B as interpretations of the achievement of the Bolshevik Party and of Lenin? (15)
2. Using Sources A to D, explain why there are different historical interpretations about the rise of the Bolsheviks and their eventual seizure of power. (30)

Worked answer

**1. ['How different' requires a response in terms of scale. There are five possibilities. These are the two extremes of 'entirely' and 'not at all', neither of which allows for genuine discussion. There is the option of sitting on the fence or of coming down on the side of 'slightly but not much', neither of which makes much sense in the context of the Sources. The most feasible option is 'largely but not entirely'. An effective approach would be to show any common ground but to go on to show that this is used for very different purposes.]*

Extracts A and B differ fundamentally in their assessment of the achievements of the Bolshevik Party. Source A provides an uncompromising eulogy to the Party, while Source B's comments are more double-edged, with a strong critical tone behind the description of some of the Party's strengths. This is to be expected from sources of such divergent origins. Source A uses history to uphold a political system, while Source B adopts a more distinctively academic approach while simultaneously showing some hostility in its analysis.

There is some common ground, but it is limited to the obvious proposition that the Bolsheviks succeeded because they were stronger than their opponents. Source A uses such words as 'overthrew' and 'smashed', while Source B refers to 'Bolshevik ascendancy' and their ability to 'neutralise' their enemies; both Sources show that the Bolsheviks were able to 'accomplish' their objective.

On the other hand, the main thrust of the two arguments is very different: Bolshevik strengths are interpreted in contrasting ways. One is the question of popularity. Source A maintains that the Bolsheviks were widely representative of the 'masses', of the 'workers' and 'peasants' (who, between them, accounted for the vast majority of the population of Russia). Source B, by contrast, claims that the 'Bolshevik Revolution was not a majoritarian movement' and that the elections to the Constituent Assembly confirmed that they had the support 'of not more than 25 per cent'. Thus Bolshevik strength was turned into 'achievement' in different ways. In Source A the Bolsheviks were seen as enablers and facilitators, as the means of 'mobilising' and 'preparing' the latent power of the people. Source B has the opposite perspective: that the Bolsheviks acted *against* the masses, applying pressure at key points to 'neutralize their opposition' and take advantage of their 'apathy'.

Finally, there is a considerable difference in how the role of Lenin is perceived. Although Source A does not refer to him explicitly, there is a strong implication that the driving force behind Bolshevik popularity and Bolshevik success was Lenin's ideology, the 'triumph of Marxism–Leninism'. Source B makes more sustained references to Lenin, but in a very different context. He is shown to be entirely pragmatic, with a self-proclaimed emphasis on 'organization' and a 'preponderance of force' at the 'decisive moment' and in the 'decisive points'. Source A therefore provides a picture of a mainstream party using the ideas of its leader to lead the masses to victory, while Source B reveals a conspirator skilfully exploiting the masses to win power for a minority.

3

THE ORIGINS AND GROWTH OF MARXISM IN RUSSIA TO 1905

BACKGROUND

Marxism made its appearance in Russia during the early 1880s, as an alternative revolutionary ideology to populism; unlike the latter, it was based mainly on the urban workers. In 1898 the various Marxist groups united to form the Russian Social Democratic Labour Party (RSPLD), under the leadership of Lenin, Martov and an ex-populist, Plekhanov. The RSDLP was committed to ending the Tsarist regime and to the eventual establishment of a workers' state. In Marxist terms this would involve the end of capitalism and of the bourgeoisie and the introduction of the 'dictatorship of the proletariat' – which would lead eventually to the 'classless society'. The Party developed a propaganda structure and the newspaper *Iskra* (*The Spark*).

Before long, however, the Russian Social Democrats began to follow the same course as their Marxist equivalent in Germany, the SPD. Differences emerged between Lenin and other leading Social Democrats, especially Martov, on questions of organisation and strategy. These surfaced at the second Congress of the RSDLP (1903), which started in Brussels and was then reconvened in London. From the bitter debates emerged two factions, soon to become parties in their own right. The Bolsheviks supported Lenin's strategy of a party organisation based on strict discipline, operated by professional revolutionaries and avoiding collaboration with other opponents of the Tsarist regime. The Mensheviks, by contrast, favoured the more democratic approach to membership advocated by Martov, along with a period of co-operation with liberals and other members of the bourgeoisie. The key question was which of the Bolsheviks and Mensheviks were to develop the more appropriate strategy. After all, Russia's unique social and political conditions meant that Marx and Engels had never even considered it as a possibility for early revolution.

ANALYSIS (1): WHY DID A MARXIST MOVEMENT DEVELOP IN RUSSIA, BUT THEN SPLIT INTO TWO FACTIONS IN 1903?

The emergence of a Marxist movement occurred mainly in the late 1880s and the 1890s, with the various groups uniting in 1898 to form the Russian Social Democratic Labour Party (RSDLP). It derived most of its support from the urban proletariat, or industrial workers. This was in contrast to the Socialist Revolutionaries who were formed in 1900 from the populist groups representing the rural proletariat, or peasantry. By 1903, however, the RSDLP had split into two main factions because of internal differences over the interpretation of Marxist ideology and its relevance to party organisation and revolutionary strategy.

The Marxists were not the original revolutionary grouping within Russia; they were preceded by the populists, who had developed during the reign of Alexander II (1855–81). But the intention of populist factions such as Land and Liberty and People's Will had been to bring radical change to the countryside by ending the social dominance of the nobility and creating communal ownership of the land. This had little relevance to the urban and industrial sector, which expanded rapidly between 1888 and 1904, the second half of the reign of Alexander III and the first decade of that of Nicholas II. Industrialisation was a deliberate policy of Sergei Witte, Finance Minister between 1893 and 1903, and was pursued with the full support of the Tsarist regime. Witte's emphasis on heavy industry, steel, oil and railways meant a rapid increase in the urban and industrial workforce. Because this happened so quickly, there was an inevitable deterioration in living conditions and an increase in urban squalor, creating an ideal breeding ground for urban radicalism. Although industrialisation was not new to Russia, its pace brought it more into line with the experience of more advanced economies in Western and Central Europe, where similar side-effects had led to the growth of movements based on Marxism, a political philosophy that developed as a reaction to the exploitation of a new industrial working class by a capitalist bourgeoisie. The template did not quite fit Russia, where the bourgeoisie were less developed than the nobility, but at least it seemed more relevant to the cities than did the rural focus of the Socialist Revolutionaries.

In other countries the growth of Marxism was contained by pressures for social reform exerted by political parties or, alternatively, by the initiative of reforming governments. Before 1905 Russia had neither. Although there were constitutional and social reformists, their activities were limited to the provincial assemblies, or *zemstva*, since neither Alexander III nor Nicholas II had any intention of establishing a central legislature. Nor did they propose to use their autocratic powers to repeat the reforming experiment of Alexander II, who had, after all, been assassinated for his pains in 1881. As a result, Marxism had an instant appeal to those who had no other form of political or social redress.

The situation was made more dangerous by the ban placed by the Tsarist regime on trade unionism, which meant the expression of any grievances was automatically considered subversive. Potential trade unionists were therefore likely to be revolutionary and, as such, were open to revolutionary ideas from abroad. There was no shortage of intellectuals familiar with the works of Karl Marx, and it so happened that *Das Kapital* was translated into Russian even before it appeared in English or French editions.

Russian Marxism was also partly of domestic origin. Although in some ways the two movements were very different, there was nevertheless some cross-fertilisation between Marxism and populism. Two revolutionary intellectuals, Akselrod and Plekhanov, became disillusioned with what they saw as the limitations of populism. Plekhanov, for example, broke with Land and Liberty in 1879, arguing that it was too constraining in its belief that socialism could be achieved only through the peasant commune. He also came to the conclusion that the tactics of terror needed to be replaced by more systematic organisation, which he set up in 1883 as the Emancipation of Labour. Other Marxist groups sprang up, engaging in ever more active disputation with the populists, absorbing some of their ideas while rejecting others. Gradually these groups merged into the Fighting Union for the Liberation of the Working Class (1895) under Lenin and Martov, which in turn linked with Plekhanov's Emancipation of Labour in 1898 to form the Russian Social Democratic Labour Party.

Until 1903 this was, in theory at least, a group united by a common ideology. After that date, however, the RSDLP effectively operated as two distinct parties – the Bolsheviks and the Mensheviks. The reasons for this schism were partly to be seen in the underlying problems of

Russian Marxism itself, and partly in the specific disputes over policy and strategy that surfaced in 1903.

Russian Marxism had several background difficulties that made some sort of break highly likely sooner or later. One was related to the complexity of the ideology and the lack of clear direction as to how to apply it. Wherever Marxist parties developed in Europe, they tended to divide between hardline revolutionaries on one wing and more cautious 'revisionists' on the other. The German Social Democratic Party (SPD) was one example of this, torn between those who wanted to overthrow the German political and social system as quickly as possible and those who thought it more realistic to try to reform it over a longer timescale. Similar trends were to occur in France, Britain and Italy – so why not Russia?

A second underlying problem was that the cross-fertilisation between Russian revolutionary movements had a negative effect on Russian Marxism. The populists went through their experience of splits and disputes before 1900, eventually achieving a degree of unity as Socialist Revolutionaries. Part of the reason for this was that their dissidents tended to join the Marxist groups, where they sought an outlet for their changing ideas. Partly as a result of their stimulus, Marxism developed rapidly and discovered a common path more quickly than did the populists. In a sense, however, the growth of Marxism had proved too rapid: unlike the Socialist Revolutionaries, the Social Democrats disintegrated after their formation. The Socialist Revolutionaries were what was left after the tensions within populism had run their course. The RSDLP, by contrast, was the battleground for future conflicts.

The radical and moderate factions of the RSDLP gradually polarised under the leadership of Lenin and Martov. Although Lenin's role may have been exaggerated in the formation of the original Marxist movement in Russia, he contributed extensively to the increase in its revolutionary momentum, partly through assertive – at times aggressive – leadership, and partly through his writings which adapted Marxist ideology to Russian conditions. These included *The Development of Capitalism in Russia* (1899), *What Is to Be Done?* (1902) and *One Step Forward, Two Steps Back* (1904). In *What Is to Be Done?* he made it clear that he favoured a disciplined and carefully organised approach to revolutionary activity. The structure of the revolutionary party should be tightly knit, conspiratorial and secretive, while the membership should consist of professional revolutionaries. Martov's position was more ambivalent. In his *Struggle with the State of Siege in the RSDLP* (1904) he later explained that he had doubts about Lenin's ideas and that he preferred a more open, democratic and evolutionary approach to achieving change;

yet, for the time being, he was prepared to avoid direct opposition for the sake of maintaining political unity. At the same time, he continued to collaborate with Lenin, Plekhanov and Akselrod, the key editorial members of the Social Democratic newspaper, *Iskra*, which had been founded in 1900. Hence the battle-lines were being drawn between 1902 and 1903, although Martov declined at this stage to accept Lenin's challenge.

The occasion for the break was the Second RSDLP Congress in 1903. This was convened in Brussels but then, because of unwelcome surveillance by the Belgian police, switched to the less constrained venue of a public house in Tottenham Court Road in London. Here the key issues of organisation and membership were raised in a more direct and confrontational manner, Lenin coming across to the moderates as overbearing and intolerant in his attitude. His personal influence may well have been an important factor in the break, since it was a sudden change to the usual working methods of revolutionaries in exile – correspondence and pamphleteering. At all events Lenin certainly created an impression. Trotsky, who was to be Lenin's right-hand man in 1917, referred in 1903 to his 'malicious suspiciousness' and considered that Lenin was 'a caricature of Jacobin intolerance'. It is also possible that Lenin felt that the Social Democrats were losing their opportunity for revolutionary action – that back in Russia the wave of strikes that had broken out in 1903 hinted that the industrial workers might try to introduce a revolution without the revolutionaries. Whatever the explanation, Martov and others, including Plekhanov, found that they could no longer accept Lenin's thesis that the organisation of the Party had to be secretive and conspiratorial, nor that the membership should be confined to professional revolutionaries. The result was the emergence of the Bolsheviks (or majority) and the Mensheviks (or minority), polarising around Lenin and Martov.

Although this split was characteristic of Marxism everywhere, it occurred in Russia first and in more concrete form. The German Social Democrats did not divide until well into the First World War, when the left-wing minority seceded as the Spartacists, or Communists. A key factor in distinguishing the two factions of Russian Marxists could well have been the contrasting influence of revolutionary strategy. The Mensheviks were, in many respects, more Western in their approach and certainly considered themselves to be more genuine and orthodox Marxists. The Bolsheviks, by contrast, had deeper roots in the Russian revolutionary traditions of secrecy and conspiracy. In this way Lenin was grafting a Western model on to a Slavic base. This was to have enormous implications for the future.

Questions

1. Why did the Russian revolutionary movements split between populists and Marxists, and then between Bolsheviks and Mensheviks?
2. What had Lenin contributed to Marxism by 1903?

ANALYSIS (2): EXAMINE SOME OF THE CONTRASTING INTERPRETATIONS FOR THE DEVELOPMENT OF MARXISM IN RUSSIA AND FOR THE SPLIT OF THE RUSSIAN SOCIAL DEMOCRATS IN 1903.

It is possible to make the development of Russian Marxism to 1903 much more controversial than in the first Analysis. A wide variety of different interpretations has been given by contemporaries, politicians and historians. These views range across the political spectrum.

The development of Marxism

An area of consensus is that Marxism developed in Russia because the country was changing and the conditions were becoming more appropriate. This was mainly because of the development of heavy industry. But within this approach are two very different angles. The official Soviet view was that Marxist ideology took root because Russia was reaching the stage in the dialectical process of the class struggle where the proletariat was becoming strong enough to challenge capitalist exploitation. Non-Soviet views would focus on more practical reasons for the emergence of a second revolutionary movement in Russia. Existing populism had little to offer those who were not tied to the land, while the concentration of a new workforce in urban centres made a more attractive target in terms of Marxist recruitment and organisation.

What of the role of Lenin in the formation of Russian Marxism? Official Soviet historiography and many Western historians have emphasised his importance as a deliberate revolutionary who planned and developed a Russian adaptation of Marxism and saw it through against the influence of such contemporaries as Plekhanov and Martov. Within this framework, however, are sharp differences in the assessment of Lenin's methods.

The Soviet version is that he was the inspiration behind the unification of the Marxist study circles into the League of Struggle for the Emancipation of the Working Class and that he 'prepared the ideological ground for the amalgamation of the Social Democratic organisations into a party'.[1] This was followed by the adaptation of Marxism to Russian conditions, a role undertaken exclusively by Lenin through his ideas on Party organisation and membership. 'Lenin's views about the Party may be summed up as follows: the Party is the organising, leading and guiding force of the revolutionary working-class movement. Lenin laid down the principles of his teaching about the Party in the period when the Party was being built up.'[2] The Soviet emphasis is therefore very much on the positive and planned creation of a new system by an inspired individual. Although the Marxist version of history is essentially structured, deterministic and based on the formula of class struggle, the role of the individual in this can be crucial as a benign agent of progress. The German Marxist Klara Zetkin summed up this view: 'Splendid Marxist that he was, Lenin grasped the particular wherever and in whatever form it revealed itself, in its relation to and its bearing upon the whole.'[3]

Most Western historians have also taken the line that Lenin was a crucial element in the development of Marxism without, however, acknowledging that he was operating within a Marxist scheme. If anything, Lenin distorted Marxism and applied a distinctively Russian approach to its application. Max Eastman, for example, maintained in 1926 that 'a fundamental difference between Marx and Lenin is visible on almost every page they wrote'.[4] According to other historians, what motivated Lenin was not so much the fulfilment of the Marxist dialectic as the achievement and retention of personal power. John Keep's view in 1968 was that 'Whatever Lenin's merits as a philosopher, historian or literary critic, he was pre-eminently a politician and it was as a master of political tactics, who skilfully manipulated men and ideas to achieve power for his party, that he won his greatest success.'[5]

Why the difference between the two approaches? The Soviet version is largely polemical. As the founder of a system and a state, Lenin was revered in a way that placed him beyond the reach of historical appraisal. His achievement was so closely tied to the Marxist plan that criticism of the one would automatically mean the dilution of the other. The ideology and the justification for the Soviet regime therefore depended on maintaining the hagiography of Lenin even if this involved distortions. By contrast, Western historians could afford to take a more critical approach. The main casualty of this was the assumption that there was an automatic harmony between Marxist principle and Lenin's adaptation of Marxism to Russian conditions. Instead, there is a much stronger emphasis on the role of the individual in shaping the ideology to his own pursuit of power. This may be for a variety of reasons, ranging from a genuine revolutionary aspiration to more selfish factors.

Finally, the Western approach has also allowed for the importance of psychological factors, although these are favoured more by some historians than by others. One, developed by James White in 2001, gives particular weight to a turning point in Lenin's early life, leaving an unspoken question as to whether Lenin would have embarked upon a revolutionary career without such an event. The occasion was the execution of his brother Alexander (known as Sasha) for terrorist activity in 1887. Lenin and his sister Olga were profoundly disturbed by this development; they 'resolved that their brother's death would not be in vain and that they would serve the cause for which he had sacrificed himself – just as soon as they could discover what that cause had been'. In the meantime they were determined to 'piece together what the ideas were that had inspired Sasha to become a revolutionary'.[6] Indeed, this may well have deflected him from the more conventional career that his academic success seemed to indicate. This is very much a case of the individual responding to chance events rather than to a broader formula.

The 1903 split

The events at the 1903 Congress, which broke the Social Democrats into Bolsheviks and Mensheviks, have been widely interpreted.

Again, the Soviet view is entirely pro-Lenin. The break occurred despite Lenin's wishes. It was due to the treachery of the 'opportunists' among the Social Democrats who 'said that the Party should admit people who did not care to belong to any Party organisation, found Party discipline burdensome and wished to limit themselves to sympathy and assistance'. This was diametrically opposed to Lenin's forward-looking plans for organisation 'which accorded so well with the interests of the people and of the country's progressive development'.[7]

The alternative approach is that the Mensheviks were the progressive influence – but that they were frustrated by Bolshevik intransigence and Leninist tantrums. Rex Wade, for example, maintains that, although Martov and Plekhanov led a less united group than the Bolsheviks, by 1917 'Menshevism emerged as more genuinely democratic in spirit and with a moderate wing willing to cooperate with other political groups for reform.'[8] A similar line is taken by Orlando Figes. The Mensheviks, he considers, 'were genuinely more democratic, both in their composition and in their policies', attracting 'a broader range of people' that inclined them more towards 'compromise and conciliation with the liberal bourgeoisie'. Figes makes an additional distinction between the two groups: the Mensheviks were influenced by 'moral scruples', whereas this was not at all the case with the Bolsheviks.[9]

The debate on the role played by Lenin in the schism of the Social Democrats fits into the above views. The official Soviet line is that 1903 was, in effect, a meeting-point between an ideology and the man best suited to implement it, and that, 'in Lenin the Russian and international proletariat had an outstanding theoretician, who carried on the work and teaching of Marx and Engels'. Lenin was also 'endowed with a clear insight' into the future needs of the working class movement.[10]

A more critical view is that Lenin's personality dictated the break – that his authoritarian approach would not allow for any opposition. This is strongly put by Figes, who maintains that 'Lenin's personality was the crucial issue' and that Bolshevism was 'defined by a personal pledge of loyalty to him'.[11]

Perhaps there is an alternative to both of these Leninocentric interpretations. It could be argued that Lenin did not dictate the trend at all. Instead, he was trying to catch up with the point reached by a workforce that was becoming increasingly militant and more involved in militant strike action. This idea was first put forward by Edmund Wilson as early as 1940. He argued that the Marxists were by 1903 struggling to keep up with the insurrectionary movement taking place in Russia and that 'Lenin was driven by the urgency of getting a grasp on it before it got hopelessly away from them and plunged on a blind course.'[12]

Within the context of the rest of his book, this was one of Wilson's less substantiated comments – even, perhaps, a bold, throwaway line. Sometimes, however, a phrase like this can turn insight into foresight: in providing a new perspective on the event, the historian can anticipate a future trend of interpretation, even if this was not his intention. There was a strong tendency in the 1990s (admittedly not shared by all historians) to emphasise the sheer scale of the strikes affecting Russia in 1902 and 1903 in major cities in southern Russia, including Rostov-on-Don, Baku and Odessa, together with growing assertiveness from Russia's national minorities and from militant peasants. As a result, much more attention has been paid to the influence of meetings within factories: these can have had little to do with formal Marxist organisation at this stage, but Marxist leaders would have been aware of them. Such developments may well have influenced the outcome of the 1903 Congress. Both factions of the RSDLP felt a need to respond to the growing grass-roots pressure: the Mensheviks by integrating themselves into it; the Bolsheviks preparing themselves to lead it. The prevailing urgency is what sharpened the differences between them, not the countervailing personalities. This would be very much in line with one of the recent shifts in revisionist history to take account of influences percolating upwards as well as power filtering downwards.

The 1903 split has all the ingredients for historical controversy. It can be seen as a turning point in ideological development, with the denouement between the progressive and opportunist poles of Marxism – whichever way round these are interpreted. Or it was perhaps a time of reckoning between two personalities representing a long-term mission versus immediate opportunism, and the interests of the people versus the interests of the leadership. Again, which way round should these be interpreted? Finally, who was really dictating the momentum of revolutionary change at the time: the Marxist leaders debating resolutions at a congress or the common worker illegally on strike? Even with this combination, there are plenty of permutations for future argument.

Questions

1. Why do some historians consider that Lenin adapted Marxism, while others argue that he distorted it? Which view is correct?
2. How convincing is it to attribute the split between Bolsheviks and Mensheviks to the influence of contrasting personalities?

SOURCES

1. LENIN AND THE CREATION OF THE BOLSHEVIKS

Source A: A Soviet painting of Lenin speaking at the Second Congress of the Russian Social Democratic Labour Party in 1903.

[See following page]

Source B: Extract from Lenin's *What Is to Be Done?*,published in 1902.

An organisation of revolutionaries must primarily and chiefly comprise people whose professions consists of revolutionary activity. This organisation must inevitably be not very wide and as secret as possible. And now I maintain: (1) that no revolutionary movement can be durable without a stable organisation of leaders which preserves continuity; (2) that the broader the mass which is spontaneously drawn into the struggle, which forms the basis of the movement and participates in it, the more urgent is the necessity for such an organisation; (3) that such an organisation must consist mainly of people who are professionally engaged in revolutionary activities; (4) that, in an autocratic country, the more we narrow the membership of such an organisation, restricting it only to those who are professionally engaged in revolutionary activities, the more difficult it will be to catch such an organisation.

Source A: A Soviet painting of Lenin speaking at the Second Congress of the Russian Social Democratic Labour Party in 1903. (Courtesy the Novosti Photo Library)

Source C: Extract from *The Russian Revolution* by Sheila Fitzpatrick, published in 1994.

In the years after 1903, the Mensheviks emerged as the more orthodox in their Marxism, less inclined to force the pace of events towards revolution and less interested in creating a tightly organized and disciplined revolutionary party. They had more success than the Bolsheviks in attracting support in the non-Russian areas of the Empire, while the Bolsheviks had the edge among the Russian workers . . .

The Bolsheviks, unlike the Mensheviks, had a single leader, and their identity was in large part defined by Lenin's ideas and personality. . . Lenin differed from many other Russian Marxists in seeming actively to desire a proletarian revolution rather than simply predicting that one would actually occur. This was a character trait that would surely have endeared him to Karl Marx, despite the fact that it required some revision of orthodox Marxism.

Questions

*1. Using Source A, and your own knowledge, explain briefly the outcome of the 1903 Congress of the RSDLP. (5)
2. To what extent do Sources A and C explain the background to and issues of Source B? (8)
3. Using Sources A–C, and your own knowledge, explain the importance of Lenin in the establishment of the Bolsheviks as a revolutionary organisation. (12)

Worked answer

**1.* [Focus on the outcome of the Congress. 'Source A' and 'own knowledge' can be dealt with separately or integrated. This answer integrates them, extracting key themes from the Source and using own ideas to explain and develop them.]*

The outcome of the 1903 Congress was a split within the Russian Social Democratic Labour Party into two factions. One of these was the Bolsheviks, led by Lenin, the other the Mensheviks under Martov. This followed a debate in London, as shown in Source A; the venue depicted was a public house in Tottenham Court Road, which would have encouraged a very intense atmosphere. It is also possible to deduce from the Source that Lenin succeeded in persuading a number of other delegates to support his strategy for the future development of the Party. Additional knowledge confirms that this strategy involved confining membership to professional revolutionaries, who would operate in secrecy under tight, centralised discipline. Since the Source is a polemical illustration, it suggests that Lenin won the day through argument. In fact, other accounts maintain that he got his way through imposing an autocratic style of leadership, in contrast to the more reasonable and democratic approach of Martov.

2. WHAT CAUSED THE SPLIT BETWEEN THE BOLSHEVIKS AND MENSHEVIKS IN 1903?

Source D: An exchange between Lenin and Martov at the Second Congress of the Russian Social Democratic Labour Party (RSDLP) in 1903.

Martov: The more widely the title of 'member of the party' is spread, the better. We can only rejoice if every striker, every demonstrator, is able to declare himself a party member.

Lenin: It is better that ten real workers should not call themselves party members than that one chatterbox should have the right and opportunity to be a member.

Source E: A recollection of the 1903 Congress by Lydia Dan, a representative who supported Martov.

I felt that I had to support him [Martov]. And many others felt that way. Martov was poorly suited to be a leader. But he had an inexhaustible charm that attracted people. It was frequently difficult to account for why they followed him. He himself said, 'I have the nasty privilege of being liked by people.' And, naturally if something like a schism occurred, Martov would be noble, Martov would be honourable, while Lenin – well, Lenin's influence was enormous. For my own part, it was very tragic to have to say that all my sympathies for Lenin (which were considerable) were based upon a misunderstanding.

Source F: Extract from Orlando Figes, *A People's Tragedy: The Russian Revolution 1891–1924*, published in 1996. At the time of publication, Figes was a lecturer in History at Trinity College, Cambridge.

For several years the incipient political differences between the Mensheviks and the Bolsheviks continued to be masked by personal factors . . . Lenin's personality was the crucial issue. Bolshevism was defined by a personal pledge of loyalty to him; and Menshevism, though to a lesser extent, by opposition to him. Lenin reinforced this divide by his violent attack on the Mensheviks in his pamphlet

One Step Forward, Two Steps Back (1904). He now called them 'traitors' to the Marxist cause. None of his Bolshevik lieutenants was even allowed to talk to any of the Menshevik leaders without gaining his prior approval.

Source G: Extract from Edmund Wilson, *To the Finland Station* (1940) on the 1903 Congress.

The crucial division took place at the Second Congress of the Social Democrats in the summer of 1903 . . . The atmosphere was terribly strained: political conflicts were wrecking personal relations. Lenin himself was so keyed up that he could hardly sleep or eat . . . When the congress was over, he collapsed.

But he won. 'Of such stuff are Robespierres made,' said Plekhanov to one of the minority. His chief opponent was his old ally, Martov. Martov, on the testimony of his antagonists themselves, was an exceptionally gifted man. Gorky calls him 'amazingly attractive'. His intelligence was penetrating and subtle; and he had, says Krupskaya, 'shown a keen sense for grasping Ilyich's ideas and developing them in a talented manner' . . . His revolutionary instincts were real; but they were subject to Hamlet-like let-downs . . . Describing him on a later occasion, Gorky says that he was 'deeply affected by the tragic drama of the dissension and split. He trembled all over, swayed backward and forward, spasmodically unfastening the collar of his starched shirt and waving his hands about.'

The split came about ostensibly over a mere clause in the programme for the party which Plekhanov and Lenin had prepared. Martov wanted to admit to the party all the liberals who might think themselves in sympathy with it; Lenin insisted on restricting it to persons who could work actively and submit to discipline. He knew that discontent in Russia was mounting up to a crisis – which came in 1905. The peasants, crushed with debts and starving . . . had been raiding and burning the manor houses and demanding a distribution of the land . . . At the moment when the congress was held, a gigantic general strike was taking place in the South of Russia. The insurrectionary movement was going ahead so fast that the Marxists had hardly been able to keep up with it; and Lenin was driven by the urgency of getting a grasp on it before it got hopelessly away from them and plunged on a blind course.

Questions

*1. How far does Source F confirm the impressions of Lenin's personal influence given in Sources D and E? (15)

2. Using Sources D to G, consider the view that clashes of personality were less important than other factors in the split among the Social Democrats at the 1903 Party Congress. (30)

Worked answer

**1. [Find criteria that will enable a direct comparison to be made between the Sources and avoid descriptive narrative. Although this question is primarily on Sources, try to include at least one historiographical reference.]*

The extent to which Source F confirms the impressions of Lenin's personal influence provided in the other two Sources depends very much on the criteria used.

As a direct description of Lenin's influence, Source F has more to add than either D or E. Source D, by contrast, provides a more neutral approach because it is confined to recording the strategies of Martov and Lenin on party policy. Source E, although mainly concerned with an assessment of Martov's character, does contain a strongly expressed view of Lenin. His influence is described simply as 'enormous'. Source F goes much further than the other two, referring to political issues being 'masked by personal factors' and Lenin's personality as 'the crucial issue'.

If more emphasis is attached to inference than to description, Sources D and E have a more obvious link with Source F. In Source D much can be deduced from the wording: Lenin's is more forceful than Martov's, especially his preference for losing 'ten real workers' than admitting 'one chatterbox'. A strong impression has also been created by Lenin on the author of Source B – even though it is a negative one ('all my sympathies for Lenin were based on a misunderstanding') and backed by no specific reason. Source F, however, completes a picture of Lenin suggested by the other two. Lenin's influence emerges through the violence of his 'attack on the Mensheviks', his use of such intemperate language as 'traitors' and his insistence on unquestioning personal loyalty.

In terms of their origins, Sources D and E have a direct connection with the 1903 Congress, the first as a transcript of what was said, the second as a recollection of the scene. The latter is bound to be more subjective than the former, but adds the type of detail that a transcript alone cannot. Source F can enhance both: it has the advantage of long-term perspective and can place the event in its immediate and longer-term context. Above all, the collapse of the Soviet Union and the emergence of 'Western revisionist' history has had the effect of removing much of the heroic (or 'evil-genius') approach to Lenin, enabling him to be presented as he may well have been – a cantankerous individual with serious character deficiencies.

4

THE BOLSHEVIKS BETWEEN 1903 AND MARCH 1917

BACKGROUND

The Tsarist regime entered a major crisis within two years of the 1903 Congress of the RSDLP. By the end of 1904 Russian forces had been defeated in the war with Japan and, in January 1905, the incident in St Petersburg known as 'Bloody Sunday' sparked a full-scale revolution, which lasted for the whole year. The main participants in this were the constitutionalists, who demanded an assembly, the urban workforce, which established the St Petersburg Soviet, and the rural peasantry in a number of provinces in European Russia. Of the revolutionary parties, the Mensheviks probably played a more direct role than the Bolsheviks, although this is debatable.

Tsarism survived by making several key concessions and dividing the revolutionaries. The October Manifesto satisfied middle-class activists by promising a constitution, and the peasantry were appeased by the promise in November to cancel their redemption payments. Now isolated, the urban revolutionaries were dealt with by the army, which, although humiliated by defeat in Japan, had remained intact.

The period between 1905 and 1914 saw a number of major changes in Tsarist Russia. A constitutional experiment began in 1906 with the establishment of a new state duma and the legalisation of political parties. The economy expanded rapidly and Stolypin's agricultural reforms had the clear intention of creating a wealthy upper stratum of peasants who would provide social stability. Although there were also powerful political and social tensions, created at least in part by the Tsar's attempt to reassert autocracy, this was not a happy period for the Bolsheviks. The split with the Mensheviks widened and became permanent, and the period to 1914 was taken up with bitter recrimination between the two groups. Although the Bolsheviks claimed the credit for widespread strike action in 1912 and 1913, there is considerable evidence that this was largely spontaneous; the influence of the Bolsheviks was, to say the least, questionable.

Russia's involvement in the First World War destabilised the whole Tsarist system. This was due largely to early military reverses at the hands of the Germans and the decision made by Nicholas II to leave Petrograd to take over the command of the armed forces in 1915. The resulting power vacuum at the centre of the regime was filled by the Tsarina Alexandra and Rasputin who, between them, managed to antagonise virtually every class, sector and interest in Russia. This was particularly productive for the various revolutionary groups, who sought to take full advantage of the regime's predicament. However, co-operation between them was another matter. The Bolsheviks kept strictly to their own devices and Lenin was in exile in Switzerland until April 1917.

The point of crisis was reached in February 1917, when the Progressive Bloc in the Duma at first put pressure on the Tsar to concede fundamental political reforms and then co-operated with the revolutionaries in Petrograd. The Tsar was forced to abdicate and the Duma established a new provisional government – at the same time that the popular insurrectionists had set up a new soviet in Petrograd, modelled on that of 1905. Whether the Bolsheviks played any part in any of these developments is considered below.

ANALYSIS (1): HOW IMPORTANT A PART DID THE BOLSHEVIKS PLAY IN THE COLLAPSE OF THE TSARIST REGIME?

The regime that the Bolsheviks brought down was a post-Tsarist one – the Provisional Government. Yet most of their formative years were spent during the Tsarist era and their subsequent claim was that they were instrumental in the destruction of both systems.

In theory the Bolsheviks played a considerable role in undermining the Tsarist system and in developing the means whereby working-class radicalism could be articulated. This, however, was within the scope of a broader aim, which was to destroy not only Tsarism but capitalism. This can be seen in a number of ways, from the inception of the Russian Social Democratic Labour Party in 1900 to the split with the Mensheviks at the Seond Congress in 1903.

In the first place the Bolsheviks formulated a strategy in which the long-term aim – the 'dictatorship of the proletariat' – determined the approach to the short-term aim – the overthrow of Tsarism. This depended on accelerating the way in which the Marxist dialectic operated by pulling down as quickly as possible the regime that followed Tsarism. It was therefore undesirable to collaborate with the bourgeoisie since they would be demolished by an alliance between the proletariat and the peasantry. This could be interpreted as a powerful revolutionary weapon, adapted by Lenin from an ideology that was originally more suitable for a more advanced state such as Germany. The Mensheviks, by contrast, had the more limited focus of collaboration with any party or group willing to oppose the Tsarist regime.

The second theoretical advantage offered by the Bolshevik approach was the preparation of a revolutionary organisation specially geared to achieving a breakthrough as quickly as possible. All the details were provided in Lenin's *What Is to Be Done?* (1902). If the dialectic were to be accelerated, the party defining the new pace had to be disciplined and centralised. Given the competition with other opposition groups such as the constitutionalists and the Socialist Revolutionaries, and also the success of the Tsarist Okhrana secret police in penetrating these groups, it made sense to operate on a professional, secretive and conspiratorial basis.

Third, the Bolsheviks developed a strategy that was able to take advantage of the war into which Russia was plunged in 1914. The basis of the conflict fitted well into Lenin's interpretation of the dialectic. In *Imperialism: The Highest Stage of Capitalism* Lenin argued that the growth of capitalism had been so rapid that the European powers had been forced into imperial expansion with the inevitable result that they had come into conflict with each other. As Russia was one of the powers involved, it made sense to work for its defeat since this would bring down the Tsarist regime as the first step to the collapse of capitalism. The Bolsheviks, it would seem, were well placed to prepare for this eventuality since their conspiratorial approach was geared up for it.

In aiming at the target beyond the Tsar, therefore, the Bolsheviks had a greater chance of success against the latter. Or did they?

It is possible that the Bolshevik approach, which affected their overall strategy and their attitudes to other parties, weakened any contribution they could have made to the collapse of the Tsarist regime. In refusing to collaborate with other opponents of Tsarism, they abandoned a perfectly viable and orthodox Marxist approach, as adopted by the Mensheviks, for one that was inflexible and divisive. The extent of the damage caused by this can be seen in the 1905 Revolution. While the Mensheviks and Socialist Revolutionaries were prepared to make common cause with the 'bourgeois' constitutionalists, the Bolsheviks played virtually no part in the strikes, mutinies and rural uprisings of 1905; nor did they have a hand in establishing the St Petersburg Soviet, the revolutionary organisation later adopted by the Bolsheviks as their own. While Lenin claimed that the experience of 1905 was that the bourgeoisie would always betray those who joined forces with them, it could equally be argued that such a strategy was the only hope of overthrowing Tsarism. Both the Mensheviks and Socialist Revolutionaries realised that the Tsarist regime, which had survived in 1905, was too strong to be brought down by another attempt at direct action, especially in view of the agricultural reforms of Stolypin and the greater concessions allowed for the development of trade unionism. This is why the Mensheviks and SRs were more willing to co-operate with the Constitutional Democrats in the Duma. It could well be that the government was far more fearful of the damage that could be done by a broad-fronted opposition than by the hardline strategy of the Bolsheviks: this is almost certainly the reason for the government's change to the Electoral Law in 1907.

What of the Bolshevik claim that they enabled workers to develop a disciplined approach to organisation and strike action? Certainly they claimed the credit for the wave of industrial unrest that hit Russia between 1912 and 1914. Recent research, however, has shown that strikes in factories and on the Lena goldfields was organised more spontaneously at local level, as were any uprisings in the countryside. Indeed, the population were more politically aware than has often been assumed. This meant that there was less need to channel their activities than to diversify and link them – which is another argument in favour of the broader strategy of the Mensheviks. The practical effect of the Bolshevik approach to the war was also limited. The enormous increase in strike action from 1915 was not directed by Bolshevik cells, although recognisably Bolshevik catchphrases were used. Nor did the Bolsheviks destroy the Tsar's armies: most mutinies were eruptions spontaneously organised by troops radicalised by experience and trauma rather than by ideological conviction. Of course, Lenin was completely uninvolved personally, leaving Geneva only in April 1917.

There is so far little evidence that Bolshevik theories, organisation and strategies had much to do with undermining Tsarism. They had even less to do with its immediate collapse. The way in which the Tsar was forced to abdicate was far more related to the 'broad opposition' approach than to 'professional conspiracy'. Indeed, it could be said that all the main ingredients of the February revolution were Bolshevik-free. The strikes in the Putilov steel works were largely spontaneous, the only significant organised group being the Mezhraiontsy, Social Democrats rather than Bolsheviks or Mensheviks. These issued proclamations and placards on 23 and 24 February urging strikes and revolt. Even these did no more than contribute to the outbreak of strike action. The hunger marches were more closely related to demonstrations on the occasion of International Women's Day, and the desertion of the Petrograd Garrison was an on-the-spot decision.

What turned these events into a change of regime again had nothing to do with the Bolsheviks. It was due much more the broadening of opposition through co-operation across classes and parties – exactly the opposite of what the Bolsheviks advocated. The Cadets and Octobrists in the Duma, sensing the inevitability of the collapse of Nicholas II, took steps to form a provisional committee, which, in turn, forced the Tsar's abdication. Meanwhile, the Socialist Revolutionaries and Mensheviks were moving in two directions. One was involvement in the Petrograd Soviet alongside the non-party delegates who had set up the soviet in the first place. The other was a broader willingness among some of their leaders, such as Kerensky and Chernov, to establish links between the soviet and the Provisional Committee. This meant that some of the deputies in the soviet also became, through the Menshevik and Socialist Revolutionary party structures, members of the Provisional Government. As a strategy for bringing down the Tsar, what could have made more sense at the time? The Progressive Bloc in the Duma could not have acted without the spontaneous uprising. The spontaneous uprising would have lacked any structure in the Petrograd Soviet without the involvement of the Mensheviks and Socialist Revolutionaries. And the Socialist Revolutionaries and Mensheviks needed the Duma as a means of establishing a broader-based regime.

Conclusions

The absence of the Bolsheviks in all this shows that their strategy had little to do with the end of Tsarism. What Bolshevik strategy did do, however, was to prepare for the next round, which was the destruction of the broad-based regime set up in March. The Bolsheviks were therefore much stronger at destroying fellow-revolutionaries than they were at overthrowing established systems.

Questions

1. Did the Bolsheviks achieve anything between 1905 and March 1917?
2. How effective was Lenin's leadership between 1905 and January 1917?

ANALYSIS (2): CONSIDER AND EXPLAIN THE DIFFERENT INTERPRETATIONS OF THE ROLE OF LENIN AND THE BOLSHEVIKS IN THE DEVELOPMENT OF REVOLUTIONARY ACTIVITY IN RUSSIA BETWEEN 1905 AND MARCH 1917.

Over the development of the Bolsheviks as a distinct group by 1903 there is a certain common ground. This, however, is more difficult to discern when we consider the years between 1905 and 1914. This was a more complex period and it is difficult to see precisely how the Bolsheviks contributed to the revolutionary activity that undoubtedly existed. As a result, there is perhaps more scope for historical 'creativity', or even 'distortion'. This is because any interpretation needs to make some sense of the confusion in order to provide a coherent explanation. Or it needs to give an emphasis that is politically acceptable to the regime that eventually followed.

The 1905 Revolution and its lessons

There are, for example, very different explanations of the part played by the Bolsheviks in the 1905 Revolution.

The official Soviet view attributed its outbreak to the 'correctness of Bolshevik tactics'. They 'were the first to engage in struggle, rallied the masses and led them with superb courage'. Unfortunately, there was still 'a lack of harmony in the actions taken by the proletariat'. This was due to the Mensheviks, who 'continued disorganising the ranks of the fighters.' There were, however, important indications of co-operation between the proletariat and the peasantry, and of the impact of the revolution abroad.[1] The official Soviet biography of Lenin provides a more dialectical view. The 1905 Revolution was the struggle against feudalism by a 'bourgeois–democratic' combination. Here, it was argued, the Bolsheviks and Mensheviks took different lines. The Bolsheviks believed that the process should be accelerated by the proletariat allying with the peasantry rather than the bourgeoisie and that the 'bourgeoisie should be pushed aside and isolated from the masses and the lie given to its so-called democracy'. But the Mensheviks destroyed the prospect of success by looking to the bourgeoisie for leadership. They did not believe in an alliance with the peasantry and were strongly opposed to an armed uprising. 'Lenin showed that the Menshevik line was a betrayal of the revolution, a striving to place the proletariat under the leadership of the bourgeoisie.' He also showed the way to future organisation through the Soviets, which he 'regarded as organs of the armed uprising and the embryo of the people's government'.[2]

Non-Soviet historians view all this as an unusually severe distortion of events. James D. White and many others have shown that the 1905 Revolution was largely a spontaneous uprising and that Lenin was unimportant. After all, he spent most of 1905 in Geneva, returning briefly to Russia only in November. At no time did he or the Bolsheviks direct the revolutionaries: indeed, 'most of the workers, peasants and soldiers who took part in the strikes, uprisings and mutinies belonged to no party and were organised by no party organisation'.[3] As for the Soviets, Christopher Hill (who is generally sympathetic to Lenin) maintains that 'the Bolsheviks played no part in their origins and little in their development'.[4] Other historians have pointed out that they owed much more to Trotsky who, at this stage, identified more with the Mensheviks than with the Bolsheviks. For this reason, Lenin was far from enthusiastic about the Soviet as an institution for future Communist rule. If anything, he considered it inferior to the Party as a means of organising working-class activism.

The differences in interpretation over the 1905 Revolution are also reflected in the lessons learned by the Bolsheviks by its failure. Superficially, there is some common ground. All views are based to some extent on the need to try to recapture the revolutionary initiative after the recovery of the Tsarist regime by the end of 1905. Logic pointed to the reunification of the Social Democrats and reconciliation between Lenin and Martov. Their responses to events, however, perpetuated and widened the split between them. At this point opinions diverge as to who was to blame for the various groups' inability to unite and overthrow Tsarism.

Soviet historians placed the whole blame on the 'opportunists' who betrayed the working class in 1905. The Mensheviks then attempted a 'reconciliation with the reactionary regime existing in tsarist Russia and with bourgeois ideology'. This meant their 'renunciation of the revolutionary struggle'. Much as he wanted to reunite the Social Democrats, Lenin 'came out strongly against any glossing over of fundamental disagreements on basic issues of the revolution'. As for Trotsky, he hampered the 'fight for a strong revolutionary party' by taking up the cause of the 'liquidators' and building 'an anti-Leninist bloc of anti-Party groups and trends'.[5] In every way, therefore, the lesson of 1905 was that the working class needed a single-minded party dedicated to Marxism. Any attempt at compromise with the middle class would only result in betrayal. The Mensheviks were therefore no longer Marxists and so could not be reunited with the Bolsheviks. It was a matter of maintaining ideological purity and preventing any further stab in the back in the future.

It is not difficult to see how this interpretation linked with the needs of the establishment that produced it. As a one-party state, it could hardly admit that the alternative strategy operated by the Mensheviks during and after 1905 might have had at least some validity. As a regime that had, in the 1920s and 1930s, disposed of Trotsky and all his suspected supporters, it had to vilify the man who had attempted to give spontaneous insurrection a structure. Once these needs and constraints are removed from one's analysis, alternative lessons emerge from the failure of 1905.

Non-Soviet historians put a much more positive slant on the Mensheviks. The events of 1905 confirmed that there were two types of Russian Marxism. One was becoming more broadly based and democratic. The lesson learned by the Mensheviks from 1905 was that the Tsarist system was too strong to be brought down by the working class alone and through conspiracy. What was needed was co-operation with all progressive forces, even if these were to be found in other classes and other parties. As a result, the Mensheviks were prepared to co-operate in the Duma, established in 1906, with the liberals in the bourgeois parties, especially the Constitutional Democrats and the Octobrists. The Bolsheviks made the reverse deduction. The broader their contact with other groups, the weaker would be their particular influence. This would undoubtedly weaken the influence of Lenin. Hugh Seton-Watson saw this as the key issue, since 'the quarrel between Mensheviks and Bolsheviks was largely personal. Lenin's convictions of his infallible revolutionary sense, and his implacable opposition to all who questioned his tactics, are essential factors in the split.'[6] Anthony Wood also stresses Lenin's absolute determination after 1905 to 'build up an entirely separate Bolshevik organisation whose central committee would exercise absolute control over a network of small cells throughout Russia'.[7] According to James White, even when attempts were made to reunite the RSDLP, Lenin's intolerant style of leadership made this impossible.[8]

The influence of the Bolsheviks on revolutionary activity between 1905 and 1916

The key question from 1905 is whether the Bolsheviks were able to make use of their organisational changes by extending their leadership over working-class movements. This is also highly controversial.

According to the official Soviet version, the period 1905–14 was one of patient consolidation or purposeful regrouping. The Bolsheviks consolidated the Party Central Committee, launched a new paper, *Pravda*, and sat as a separate party in the new Duma. Under Lenin's leadership, 'The Bolshevik Party headed all the manifestations and forms of the struggle of the proletariat.' The wave of strikes throughout Russia between 1912 and 1914 was the response to the Bolshevik urge 'to intensify the revolutionary struggle, which was shaking the foundations of Tsarism'. The Bolsheviks inspired first of all the protests in the Lena goldfields (1912) and then a general strike in St Petersburg. The collapse of the Tsarist regime was by now inevitable.[9]

The outbreak of the First World War provided a further opportunity, which Lenin successfully interpreted and exploited. While Social Democrats everywhere were divided over the question of whether to support the war effort, the Bolsheviks were resolute. They 'marched in the forefront of the fighters for Marxism and rallied the revolutionary forces in the international working-class movement'. By contrast, the 'opportunists' collaborated with the various governments while those who were undecided – the 'centre' – criticised the opportunists but did not make a clean break with them. The leaders of this trend were 'Karl Kautsky in Germany and Leon Trotsky in Russia'. Hence 'The Bolsheviks were the only Party which remained true to socialism and internationalism and drew up a revolutionary programme of struggle against the war.' Guided by Lenin's writings, the Bolsheviks managed to turn the 'imperialist war' into a 'civil war'; they 'headed strikes', turning them into 'political actions against tsarism.' They also organised dissent and mutinies within the army, and established links with the peasantry and the different national groups.[10]

Several comments can be made on this Soviet version. The approach has a certain underlying logic. The Bolsheviks were taking history forward in the direction dictated by the dialectical process. Their organisational changes after 1905 had enabled them (and them alone) to use the war to their advantage and to fulfil an earlier maxim of Engels that 'war is the midwife of every old society pregnant with a new one'. The problem is that this interpretation does not fit the facts, as generations of non-Soviet historians have pointed out. Rather than being a phase of consolidation for the Bolsheviks, the period 1905 to 1914 resembled rather more a time of crisis, with Lenin becoming increasingly eccentric and dictatorial in his leadership of the Bolshevik faction. As for the growth of Bolshevik control over the working-class groups, this simply did not happen. It is true that there was a wave of strikes from 1912, but these were largely spontaneous. The shooting of workers in the Lena goldfields in 1912 was very similar in its effect to the Bloody Sunday incident of 1905. But, as James White maintains, 'neither the Bolsheviks nor any of the other revolutionary parties in Russia played any noticeable part in leading the workers in this period'. For one thing, most of the leadership were in exile and had only weak links with party organisations within Russia. For another, Lenin's political manoeuvres 'served only to confuse the local Bolshevik activists, and to render them less able to give the kind of leadership the situation demanded'.[11]

There appears to be a consensus among non-Soviet historians that the period 1905–14 was not a constructive one for the Bolsheviks. Nevertheless, there is one major debate that has a bearing on how Bolshevik recovery can be interpreted. Western historians have always been divided over the future of Tsarist Russia. Did it have a realistic chance of survival only to be destroyed by the catastrophe of military defeat (as argued by the 'optimists')? Or was it foredoomed, the First World War acting as the fatal blow that despatched it (the view of the 'pessimists')?

If it was the former (optimist), then it could be argued that revolutionaries of all kinds were in trouble before 1914. The agricultural reforms of Stolypin, given time, might well have created a more stable peasantry, while the industrial revival and constitutional experiment could have led to more structured social reforms. The Bolsheviks were, however, lifted by the outbreak of war, which gave them the opportunity to convert conspiracy into active subversion both in the army and in industry.

The alternative (pessimist) approach now has the support of the recent research of the revisionists. Tsarist Russia was living on borrowed time before 1914. The agricultural and industrial reforms were insufficient to quieten the working class or the peasantry, while the middle classes were not won over by the limited nature of the constitutional experiment from 1906. The revolutionary groundswell was becoming ever stronger – but not as a result of the activities of any particular party. Far from being innately conservative, the peasantry were becoming more politically conscious and the increasing numbers who migrated to the cities in search of work were particularly radical. The industrial workforce, meanwhile, had developed layers of organisation that were related to local needs. Far from building these up, the Bolsheviks later adapted their own structure to fit them. Before the outbreak of war, therefore, there were already impending signs of revolution – but not of Bolshevik revolution.

This second approach has implications for interpreting what happened during the First World War. The war accelerated the process by weakening the Tsarist structure so much that it eventually gave way to the growing pressures from below. The Bolsheviks did not contribute very much to this. First, they were not the only revolutionary group to oppose the war effort. Most of the Mensheviks, including Martov and Plekhanov, were also anti-war, while their newspaper, *Golos* (*Voice*), blamed the conflict on the imperialism of the ruling classes, a line similar to that of Lenin in his pamphlet *Imperialism: The Highest Stage of Capitalism* and the Bolshevik periodical *Kommunist.* As for Lenin's role in 'turning the imperialist war into a civil war', this was very limited in practice. Robert Service maintains that the war isolated Lenin: 'Returning to Switzerland, he was rarely able to give effective direction to his organizations in Russia.'[12] He refused to co-operate with the other revolutionary groups, who were holding conferences at Zimmerwald and Kienthal between 1915 and 1916, and insisted on maintaining a separate Bolshevik approach.

Nor was this particularly successful. The Bolsheviks were not responsible, as has often been suggested, for the breakdown of military cohesion within the army. Evan Mawdsley and others have shown that that such breakdowns in discipline were largely spontaneous, involving the rebellion of peasant conscripts against excessively harsh discipline. The Bolsheviks 'had at the outset few supporters and virtually no members in the active forces'.[13] Industrial unrest followed a similar pattern. Although there were many strikes in 1915 and 1916, there is little evidence that these were manipulated to the Bolshevik cause. Even the Putilov works, with 20,000 workers, had only 150 Bolsheviks by February 1917.

The revolution of February 1917

By the time we reach February 1917, we have a variety of possible interpretations about the position of the Bolsheviks. No one seriously suggests that the overthrow of the Tsar was directly organised and led by Lenin, and all versions of 1917 distinguish either between two revolutions or the two stages of one revolution. But there are differences of opinion as to whether the Bolsheviks contributed anything at all to the first.

The official Soviet line was that the workers in the factories and Putilov armaments works finally revolted because they had reached the point of desperation. But their action was far from spontaneous and showed the long-term influence and effectiveness of Bolshevik organisation and strategy – even though Lenin was still abroad at the time. The problem was that the bourgeoisie became involved through the Duma and, with the full co-operation of the Socialist Revolutionaries and the Mensheviks, stole from the workers the fruit of their victory. The result was the formation of the Provisional Government as a class-based alternative to the soviet established by the workers. The Bolsheviks had to become more directly involved from April onwards to redress the balance and ensure the triumph of the proletariat in line with the Marxist dialectic.

The non-Soviet version now offers two interpretations. The more traditional view is that the Tsarist regime collapsed under the weight of its own disastrous performance in the war and because the Rasputin escapade had entirely removed any remaining political credibility. In these circumstances, with the Duma openly defiant and the situation worsened by the harshest winter of the twentieth century, there was every chance that a spontaneous eruption, in the form of food riots and women's marches, could bring down a system that had survived similar attacks on it in 1905. The workers owed little to the Bolsheviks, who had nothing to do with the formation of the Petrograd Soviet. If any organisations were involved, it was the Socialist Revolutionaries and the Mensheviks. As the Committee of the Duma tried to restore order by establishing the Provisional Government, leading SRs and Mensheviks urged the Soviet to co-operate, and some, such as Chernov and Kerensky, even joined the Provisional Government. In this process the Bolsheviks were nowhere to be seen. Lenin did not make an appearance in Petrograd until April, although from that time onwards he took advantage of the problems of the Provisional Government and masterminded a Bolshevik coup against it.

More recently, 'bottom-up' revisionism has had a considerable impact on reassessing the trends of 1917. The February Revolution was surprisingly well organised, by strike committees and soldiers' groups that had had plenty of experience with revolutionary activity. They seemed to manage perfectly well without organisation from any of the revolutionary parties, whether Socialist Revolutionaries, Mensheviks or Bolsheviks. When, however, the Provisional Government gave priority to continuing the war – and, in the process, won over the likes of Kerensky to the cause – the grass-roots organisations became increasingly disillusioned and were prepared to accept the leadership of a party that was willing to take on their cause.

Conclusion

The revisionist approach seems to be directing us towards a Bolshevik Party that from now onwards learned the need to be pragmatic rather than ideological and prepared to change its policy to fit the needs of the moment and the demands of the population. Does this theory stand up?

Questions

1. How valid are the criticisms which have been made of Lenin's leadership and revolutionary strategy between 1905 and March 1917?
2. Why is the Soviet view so insistent that the period between 1905 and 1917 was one of high achievement for the Bolsheviks?

SOURCES

1. THE SOCIAL DEMOCRATS AND THE 1905 REVOLUTION

Source A: Extract from *The Programme of the Russian Social Democratic Labour Party (Bolshevik)*, August 1903.

The most outstanding among the relics of the past, the mightiest bulwark of all this barbarism, is the tsarist autocracy. By its very nature it is bound to be hostile to any social movement, and cannot but be bitterly opposed to all the aspirations of the proletariat toward freedom.

By reason of the above, the first and immediate task put before itself by the Russian Social Democratic Workers' Party is to overthrow the tsarist autocracy and to replace it with a democratic republic . . .

To attain its immediate goals, the Russian Social Democratic Workers' Party will support every opposition and revolutionary movement directed against the existing social and political system in Russia.

Source B: Extract from Michael Lynch, *Reaction and Revolution: Russia 1881–1924* published in 1992.

It is a remarkable feature of the 1905 Revolution how minor a role was played by the revolutionaries. Hardly any of them were in St Petersburg or Moscow when it began. Revolution occurred in spite of, rather than because of, them. With the exception of Trotsky, none of the SDs made an appreciable impact on the course of events. This has led many historians to doubt whether the events of 1905 merit being called a revolution. They further point to the fact that in a number of important respects tsardom emerged from the disturbances stronger rather than weaker.

Source C: Extract from Sheila Fitzpatrick, *The Russian Revolution*, published in 1982.

With hindsight it might seem that the Marxist revolutionaries, with 1905 under their belts and 1917 already looming on the horizon, should have been congratulating themselves on the workers' spectacular revolutionary debut and looking confidently towards the future. But in fact their mood was quite different. Neither Bolsheviks nor Mensheviks had got more than a toehold in the workers' revolution of 1905: the workers had not so much rejected as outpaced them, and this was a very sobering thought, particularly for Lenin. Revolution had come but the regime had fought back and survived.

Questions

1. Using your own knowledge, explain briefly the reference in Source A to 'tsarist autocracy'. (3)

*2. With reference to your own knowledge of the Bolsheviks and Mensheviks, explain the similarities and differences between Source B and Source C over their assessment of the contribution of the Social Democrats to revolution in Russia. (7)

3. In what ways, and with what degree of success, did the Bolsheviks and Mensheviks adapt themselves between 1903 and 1916 to the task of ending 'tsarist autocracy' (Source A). (15)

Worked answer

**2. [Avoid narrative descriptions from the Sources and make sure that comparisons are direct. Do this by selecting criteria on which the Sources may be compared.]*

Sources B and C follow a similar theme, which is bound to result in at least some overlapping interpretations. Two are particularly apparent. The first is the absence of professional input into the 1905 Revolution. Source B points out 'how minor a role was played by the revolutionaries' and Source C claims that 'Neither Bolsheviks nor Mensheviks had got more than a toehold in the workers' revolution of 1905'. The other parallel is the almost complete recovery of the Tsarist system. According to Source B, it 'emerged from the disturbances stronger rather than weaker', while Source C's version is that 'the regime had fought back and survived'.

The differences between the two sources are more subtle. In the extract selected as Source B Lynch focuses more on the revival of the regime, possibly to prolong the theme of 'reaction' that plays such a prominent part in the title of his book. This would lead to the widely held interpretation that the revolutionaries, whether Bolsheviks or Mensheviks, learned from the experience of 1905, although they applied their lessons in different ways. In Source C Fitzpatrick suggests a variation to this approach – that in being 'outpaced' by the workers one of the revolutionary leaders (Lenin) might well have taken this as the greatest lesson of all. This reflects a more 'revisionist' approach to Lenin's leadership and ideas.

2. HOW IMPORTANT WERE THE BOLSHEVIKS IN STIRRING UP OPPOSITION BETWEEN 1914 AND 1917?

Source D: Extract from *A Short History of the Communist Party of the Soviet Union*. This work was prepared, under the guidance of the government of the USSR, by a committee of Soviet historians.

The struggle to implement Lenin's Manifesto in Russia made headway step by step . . . The Bolsheviks conducted most of their work among the proletariat. They exposed the government and the social-chauvinist Mensheviks and Socialist-Revolutionaries who collaborated with it, and at the factories restored the Party organisations that had been broken up by tsarism and established new ones. The Party skilfully directed the dissatisfaction of the masses against tsarism, which was responsible for all their misery. The Bolsheviks headed strikes, turning them into political actions against tsarism. They went ahead with revolutionary agitation in the Army, where the penalty for this was death, and they stirred the peasants to action. The voice of the Party was heard by the working people of the non-Russian regions as well.

As had been forecast by the Bolsheviks, tsarism began to suffer defeat at the front . . . nothing could now help tsarism. The throne was reeling. The tormented people were rising to the struggle with the proletariat at their head . . . This was an indication that the revolution was approaching rapidly. The prevision of Lenin's Manifesto about the revolution was becoming a fact.

Source E: Extract from David Fry, *Russia: Lenin and Stalin*, published in the *Men and Movements* series in 1966.

The only immediate opposition to the war in the Duma came from the Social Democrats – theoretically still a single party, but in fact split into two groups, Lenin's Bolsheviks (from a Russian word meaning 'majority man'), and the Mensheviks (from the word meaning 'minority man') – and from some of the left-wing of the Socialist Revolutionaries. All other parties and independent members united in a 'Sacred Union' to support the war. Lenin himself spent the three years until just before the revolution in exile in Switzerland.

We have just mentioned that the Social Democrats were divided into Bolsheviks and Mensheviks. This was a difference of great importance, dating back to the Party's Congress in 1903, where Lenin and his supporters had differed from another group, led by Martov. The differences between the Bolsheviks and the Mensheviks were very complicated, but in the main they were questions of how best to achieve the socialist future that both groups wanted. Lenin, soon to prove himself the best political tactician in Russia, stressed the revolutionary idea of the socialist movement, and treated politics rather like a military exercise, with the Bolsheviks as a body of trained and disciplined leaders.

This was well shown in his analysis of the war. We have seen that the Social Democrats were internationalists who believed that the working people of each country should be allies against the capitalists. If the workers refused to fight each other, this would halt the war and be a step towards the world revolution for which the Social Democrats were hoping and working. The workers should therefore oppose the war. In practice, however, the international socialist movement was split up, since most workers supported their own governments, arguing that the war was just. In Russia the Mensheviks in the Duma withdrew their opposition, and the Bolsheviks remained for some time the only group actually opposed to the war. Lenin, in exile, spent much of his time developing his ideas on war and revolution.

Source F: Extract from Rex Wade, *The Russian Revolution, 1917*, published in 2000.

The war and its economic problems both mobilized and radicalized the industrial workers. Wartime production pressures led to deteriorating working conditions, longer hours and harsher punishments for strikes or labour infractions (including being drafted and sent to the front), while the deterioration of urban services and the scarcity of foodstuffs and consumer goods affected workers as well as others of the poorer urban population. Moreover, the social, industrial and political sources of conflict that had led to the great upsurge of strikes on the eve of the war still existed. Strikes again increased as workers were able, despite wartime suppression, to use underground unions and strike organizations as well as the few legal organizations available to them as a means to keep struggling to improve their lives . . .

The deteriorating conditions in society drew the attention of the revolutionary parties as well as that of the police. The strikes of 1915–16 energized the socialist parties to capitalize on popular discontents to try to promote, even lead, any revolution that might be developing. All the socialist parties increased their activity at the factories and also at higher educational institutions and even in army garrisons. By late 1916 this had grown, in Petrograd and other large cities, into a significant presence, although broader organizational structures and leadership remained fragile even where existent at all . . .

The major socialist party leaders and theoreticians were in exile, but significant numbers of second-level leaders were in Petrograd . . . The nature and amount of activity by the socialist parties on the eve of the revolution, the extent of their contact with factory-level activists and how much influence they had on events remain frustratingly unclear. Post-Soviet archival revelations suggest that it may have been more extensive and more important than previously thought, especially by parties other than the Bolsheviks.

Questions

1. How far does Source E confirm the importance of Bolshevik opposition in the First World War shown in Source D? (15)

*2. Using Sources D to F and your own knowledge, explain why there is controversy over whether the opposition to Tsarism during the First World War was promoted by the Bolsheviks. (30)

Worked answer

*2. *[It is preferable to develop your own approach, based on 'own knowledge', and to refer to the Sources within that context. An opening paragraph might, however, identify the main differences between the Sources.]*

Source D shows Lenin's use of the First World War as crucial to the development of revolution as a long-term trend, whereas Source E considers that the war was used in a more pragmatic way by Lenin and Source F challenges the view that the Bolsheviks made any effective use of the war at all. The basic reasons for these differences lie partly in the purpose of the works from which the extracts are taken, and partly in the contrasting style of evidence used. The three Sources are representative of a broad range of views that can be supplemented by further knowledge.

The underlying motivation for the different interpretations is crucial. The official Soviet view, expressed in Source D, is based mainly on political factors, while the other two are more academic. This, in itself, is a reflection of the regimes within which the Sources were developed. The *Short History of the CPSU* was ordered by the regime with the primary purpose of justifying the latter's existence. How the First World War was interpreted played an important part in this. The Soviet system was obviously based on the victory of the Bolsheviks in October 1917. But a common anti-Soviet accusation, mainly from Western historians, was that the Bolsheviks had seized power from the Provisional Government, which was taking tentative steps towards democracy. It was therefore necessary for the Soviet regime to show that the Provisional Government had, like Tsarism, been exploiting the Russian people. This meant proving that the Provisional Government, consisting of bourgeois Constitutional Democrats, along with the 'social-chauvinist Mensheviks and Socialist Revolutionaries' (Source D), had seized the fruits of victory won by the masses in February. This victory had, in turn, to have been set up by the Bolshevik activities against the Tsarist regime during the First World War, acting in accordance with the 'prevision of Lenin' (Source D). Only in this way could there be an unbroken line between the foundation of the Bolshevik Party and the later Soviet regime.

Such an approach to Bolshevik influences during the First World War was clearly alien to any Western historians, who would not be subject to any governmental dictates or constraints. Yet there is an underlying political influence which shapes both Sources E and F and others like them. The result is rather strange. Sources E and F, produced in open societies in the West, disagree more with each other than does E with D, the product of a totalitarian regime. Source E was published in 1966, at a time when the Cold War was still in progress. Most Western historians reflected the prevailing view that the Soviet Union was an ideological contrast, or even threat, to the West. Explaining the origin of this threat meant covering much of the same ground as the Soviet interpretation that Lenin and the Bolsheviks were a powerful influence on the future. Source E, for example, shows that the key to Bolshevik success in stirring up opposition to the regime was that Lenin was 'the best political tactician', treating politics 'like a military exercise'. What differed was whether such action was positive (as stated in Source D) or negative (as inplied in Source E). By the time that Source F was written, the political climate had changed completely. The Soviet Union had collapsed and Lenin had been politically discredited and his historical significance could be reduced in proportion to his political influence. Revisionist historians therefore began to downgrade the influence of the Bolsheviks. Source F, for example, refers to the popular influences behind strikes during the First World War, along with 'parties other than the Bolsheviks'.

Another key factor in explaining the different approaches to the Bolshevik involvement in the First World War would be differing concepts of history as a process and an academic discipline. Source D reflects the Marxist view that history is part of a dialectical process, with the Bolsheviks, under Lenin's leadership, providing the channel for the uprising of the masses. This acts in accordance with a formula, based on the 'prevision of Lenin's Manifesto' (Source D). The logic of this demanded that the Bolsheviks play the role of arousing opposition to the Tsarist regime in wartime, thus confirming that war is a catalyst for revolution, or, in the Marxist phrase, 'the locomotive of history'.

Western historians tend to be suspicious of such determinism. But there can be other conceptual structures that shape historical interpretation. Source E is an example of the line that history is dominated by great individuals: this is confirmed by the Source attribution, which refers to 'the *Men and Movements* series'. The Bolsheviks developed the revolutionary situation and Lenin led the Bolsheviks. Power was therefore exercised by a small minority of 'trained and disciplined leaders' – acting from above to create opposition from below.

Recent revisionist historians have tended to adopt the opposite approach. Source F is a good example of the revisionist tendency to see power welling up from below and exerting a direct influence on leaders and movements. This can be seen in the references to 'radicalized' industrial workers, the 'great upsurge' of strikes and, above all, to the socialist parties being able to 'capitalize on popular discontents' to 'lead any revolution that might be developing'. A basic factor behind this recognition of the role of the common person is the enormous increase in historical studies based on social and local history. The result is a new perspective based on a complex picture of detailed components. It contrasts with the sharper focus on the importance of the individual leader (Source E) and leadership within the context of ideology (Source D).

5

THE BOLSHEVIKS AND THE OCTOBER REVOLUTION

BACKGROUND

After the collapse of the Tsarist regime, in March 1917 two institutions claimed political authority. One was the Petrograd Soviet, a workers' council that was elected by soldiers and labourers and consisted mainly of Menshevik and Socialist Revolutionary deputies. The other, the Provisional Government, had been set up by a committee of the Duma and was dominated by Constitutional Democrats and Octobrists under the leadership of Prince Lvov.

At first the Bolsheviks seemed comparatively insignificant. Lenin had returned from exile in Switzerland only in April 1917 and had set himself the task of trying to take over the soviet and use it to destroy the Provisional Government. For a while this seemed impossible. The Socialist Revolutionaries and Mensheviks within the Soviet were prepared to form a political partnership with the Provisional Government; this was cemented in the person of the Socialist Revolutionary Kerensky, who succeeded Lvov as head of the Provisional Government on 9 July. Earlier in the same month Lenin had been seriously embarrassed by an abortive Bolshevik uprising; he had tried to prevent it on the grounds that it was premature. The Provisional Government ordered the raiding of the Bolshevik headquarters and issued warrants for the arrest of the Bolshevik leaders. Lenin escaped this only by going into hiding in Finland. It seemed, therefore, that the Provisional Government had triumphed and that the Bolsheviks had shot their bolt.

Through much of 1917, however, the Provisional Government faced serious difficulties that eventually worked in favour of the Bolsheviks. It maintained Russia's support for the Allies but, in the process, suffered further losses of territory to the Germans from July onwards. The economy, too, was in desperate trouble and the peasantry were openly seizing the landlords' estates in many rural areas. Kerensky, hoping to preside over an orderly land transfer, sent troops to deal with peasant violence, thus antagonising a large part of the population. The Bolsheviks were able to came out openly in support of the peasants. The worst crisis confronting the Provisional Government, however, was the revolt by General Kornilov, Commander-in-Chief of the Russian army: he tried in August and September to overthrow the Provisional Government and to substitute for it a military dictatorship that he hoped would drive back the German invaders and deal with the internal threat of revolution. Kerensky could rely upon the Petrograd Soviet to mobilise support against Kornilov's troops, but he needed additional help if he were to save the Provisional Government. In desperation he turned to Bolshevik units known as Red Guards and agreed to arm them if they joined the defence of Petrograd. This decision saved the capital but placed the Provisional Government in grave peril. The liberals pulled out of the coalition with Kerensky, who was now left with a small fraction of his original support.

By October the Bolsheviks had also become the most popular alternative to the Provisional Government. They had won majorities in the Petrograd and Moscow Soviets, from which Lenin deduced that the time had come to seize the initiative and sweep Kerensky from power. The Petrograd Soviet was used as a front for Bolshevik revolutionary activity. Trotsky, its president, was also the overall co-ordinator of the impending coup, directing the activities of the newly formed Revolutionary Military Committee from his headquarters in the Smolny Institute.

From 24 to 25 October 1917 the Bolshevik Red Guards seized, with surprising ease and minimal bloodshed, the key installations of Petrograd. These included banks, telephone exchanges, railway stations and bridges. By 26 October the Winter Palace and the Admiralty Buildings, the administrative headquarters of the

Provisional Government, had also been stormed and executive power was in Bolshevik hands.

These events are explained in the next three sections. Analysis (1) outlines the three main ingredients of any interpretation of Bolshevik success, while Analyses (2) and (3) examine the different emphases given to these by historians since the event.

ANALYSIS (1): WHY WERE THE BOLSHEVIKS ABLE TO OVERTHROW THE PROVISIONAL GOVERNMENT IN OCTOBER 1917?

Bolshevik success in October 1917 can – logically – be attributed to three main possibilities. The first was the social and political situation between February and October, which gradually undermined the Provisional Government and its supporters. The second was the growing popularity of the Bolsheviks during the course of 1917, which meant that they were able to harness a powerful undercurrent of revolutionary activism. And the third was the Bolsheviks' organisation and strategy, which enabled them to take maximum advantage of the vulnerability of their opponents and the resentment of the urban and rural masses.

The weaknesses of the Provisional Government and its supporters

The underlying problem of the Provisional Government between March and October 1917 was the rivalry with the Petrograd Soviet.

The Provisional Government consisted, at first, of Constitutional Democrats and Octobrists, and stood for the development of a Western-type parliamentary system. The soviet comprised parties of the left, initially the Mensheviks and Socialist Revolutionaries. Although some members of the soviet, such as Kerensky – a Socialist Revolutionary – were drawn into the Provisional Government, such developments did not prevent the two institutions pulling apart over conflicting policies on the continuation of the war and the distribution of land. To make matters worse, there was also dissension within the Provisional Government itself: the liberals pulled out of the government in August over the Kornilov Revolt so that Kerensky was left virtually isolated, presiding over a mere rump separated from the soviet by an ever-widening gulf. The Provisional Government was, therefore, inherently unstable and would have found survival difficult even in favourable circumstances. However, its task was rendered impossible by its military commitments. In the summer of 1917 it launched a great offensive against the Germans and Austrians in Galicia. This proved a disastrous failure and from July onwards the Provisional Government faced the constant spectre of German advance. The Russian army was in imminent danger of collapse, which, in itself, caused problems: mass desertions increased the level of instability while, at the top, officers such as Kornilov felt that they had little to lose by taking matters into their own hands. All this was of enormous significance to the Bolsheviks.

In the first place the Provisional Government was an essential factor in the draining of long-standing and traditional support from other revolutionary groups. The Mensheviks had always enjoyed wider popularity than the Bolsheviks in the urban areas, while the Socialist Revolutionaries had the support of the large majority of the peasants. Both, however, were compromised by their association with the Provisional Government. The main charge against them was that they placed a higher priority on winning the war than on settling other issues such as peasant ownership of the land and the calling of a constituent assembly. Under such pressure these parties, which had always had a broader base than the Bolsheviks, began to disintegrate. One section kept faith with the coalition strategy of the Provisional Government and saw sense in prioritising the war effort. These were the majority (or Right) Socialist Revolutionaries and Mensheviks. Collectively they are often called 'Revolutionary Defencists' or 'Moderate Socialists'. The other section became more radicalised, especially after August 1917, as the Left SRs and the Menshevik Internationalists. These became increasingly conscious of the problem of pursuing the policy of the Provisional Government and the loss of popular support that this entailed.

The Bolsheviks gained directly from this confusion. They received exactly the impetus they needed to progress from a foreign-based revolutionary conspiracy to a mainstream political party. The events of 1917 provided the first major change that uniquely assisted the Bolsheviks. All previous developments, including the outbreak of war in 1914, had run more in favour of the other revolutionary groups, who had, for example, played a vital role in the February Revolution. But as support drained away from the moderates it was bound to go in the direction of the Bolsheviks: where else could it have gone? The problems of the Provisional Government itself increasingly showed the failures of its policies and strategies. These occurred in a series of highlights such as the attempted Kornilov Revolt in August. The collapse of the coalition with the Constitutional Democrats showed that even the strategy of co-operation, long favoured by the Mensheviks, was breaking down. In this situation a disillusioned public became increasingly radical, and therefore more likely respond to radical solutions. The process was assisted by the linking channels set up by the Left SRs and the Menshevik Internationalists.

The influence of the masses

Once the Mensheviks and Socialist Revolutionaries began to lose support from the population at large, the main beneficiaries were the Bolsheviks. Historians remain divided as to exactly how popular the Bolsheviks were (see Analysis (2)). But there seems little doubt that the tide was running their way – and quite possibly taking them along with it.

There was, it seems, a two-way relationship between the Bolsheviks and various groups whose loyalty normally lay elsewhere. One sector, which has in the past been greatly underestimated, was the peasantry. They provided a radical impetus, insisting on the return of the land to those who worked it, and taking action to ensure that this happened. Peasant petitions also demanded justice through peasant courts, elected local authorities and more extensive education. Although there were frequent revolts, violence was not mindless but aimed at eliminating opposition to such designs. The Bolsheviks, not normally known for their sympathy for the peasantry, hastened now to respond to their pressure. In his *April Theses* Lenin made promises on land ownership that were certainly at odds with Marxist collectivism. The urban workers also exerted pressure. The most active were the skilled workers, who tended to dominate the local soviets and factory committees, and who now also looked to the Bolsheviks. Those who had previously been more inclined towards the Mensheviks had now become radicalised by the disappointments following the February Revolution. Elements within the army reacted in very much the same way, demanding the democratisation of the command and an early end to the war – both of which Lenin was willing to guarantee.

This popular surge was precisely what the Bolsheviks needed. They had never been particularly popular as a conspiratorial party operating strictly along the lines of Lenin's principles in *What Is to Be Done?* In closing themselves off from broadly based membership they had frequently been overshadowed by the Mensheviks and their revolutionary role before 1917 was never impressive (see Chapter 4). Indeed, Lenin played no part in the events of February 1917 and did not even set foot in Russia until April. Yet, from that stage onwards, things changed. The grass-roots influences benefited the Bolsheviks in several ways, forcing them to become, for the first time, a widely representative party. This in turn meant that the Bolsheviks responded to the situation between April and October 1917 with greater flexibility than they had to any previous crisis. Lenin was prepared to make substantial concessions by meeting popular demands halfway in his *April Theses*. In the process the Bolsheviks established contact with other disillusioned radicals, such as the Left SRs and the Menshevik Internationalists, thus widening the splits among their old revolutionary rivals.

The organisational strengths of the Bolsheviks

Much has now been written about the organisation and leadership of the Bolsheviks (see Analysis (2)). The starting point, however, has to be that the Bolsheviks were the group ultimately to take advantage of the weakness of its opponents and to respond to the growing radicalism of the masses. For this they must have had an organisation that was appropriate to the demands placed upon it.

An common argument now is that the Bolsheviks did not need to be effectively organised, since they rode to power on a wave of popular resentment (see Analysis (2)). They were in a stronger position than their rivals – the Socialist Revolutionaries and the Mensheviks – who had sacrificed much of their credibility in 1917 by urging support for the policies of the Provisional Government. The Bolshevik Party was more democratic and decentralised than is often realised – precisely because this was the best way of adapting to the goals of several different sectors of society. It has therefore been argued that the Bolsheviks represented the general revolutionary trend in 1917 more effectively than any of the other parties precisely because they were *not*, at this stage, a centralised and conspiratorial organisation.

Such interpretations are based partly on new research and partly on a new emphasis. They should be considered but do not have to be accepted in full. It is still possible at least to consider the more traditional view that the Bolsheviks were centrally focused. Lenin himself had for many years emphasised the need for a tight party with a core of people engaged in revolution as a profession. Admittedly these were in disagreement in October 1917 as to the timing of the revolution, but they did not split the Bolshevik Party into two parts, as happened to the Mensheviks and Socialist Revolutionaries, because – when it came to the crunch – they rallied behind Lenin. Leadership has to be based on several principles. One is acknowledgement of popular pressures and influences. Lenin, as we have seen, was open to this. Another is the willingness to force colleagues into a course of action with which they did not agree. There was still enough of the autocrat in Lenin for him to be able to do this.

While allowing Lenin his place, we should not, however, lose sight of the balancing effect of revisionist ideas. A reasonable synthesis might go as follows. The Bolsheviks were not at this stage imposing their will on the people, nor were they shaping the revolution to their own design. Their organisation was therefore not essential for creating support for revolution. However, it was necessary to enable Lenin to motivate the rest of the Central Committee into taking action. It has been argued that the decision to overthrow the Provisional Government was precipitated by Kerensky's attempt at a pre-emptive strike against the Bolshevik headquarters. This may well be true. Even so, many leading Bolsheviks preferred to wait until the calling of the first Congress of Soviets. This was imminent and would have added widespread legitimacy to Bolshevik action. In any case Kerensky was known to have very little military support. The fact that Lenin was prepared to take action before the meeting of the Congress of Soviets and against the views of some of his colleagues does seem to indicate a disciplined and autocratic party structure – whatever other adjustments it had made since April 1917.

Conclusion

The convergence of the three factors considered above was unique to the second half of 1917. Before then the Bolsheviks lacked a popular power-base and their organisation counted for comparatively little in the face of the more extensive support given to their rivals. After that date these rivals began to recover some of their losses and the Bolsheviks had to respond by becoming more repressive and therefore less responsive to popular opinion. But, for the brief period between April and October 1917, the three trends came together. The Bolsheviks were able to adapt their organisation to respond to popular pressures that, in turn, had been created by the crisis of the other parties – compromised as they were by their association with a failing Provisional Government.

Questions

1. Why were the Bolsheviks able to rise from comparative insignificance before April 1917 to become masters of Russia by October?
2. How important was the personal role of Lenin in the Bolshevik Revolution?

ANALYSIS (2): EXPLAIN AND ACCOUNT FOR THE DIFFERENT INTERPRETATIONS OF THE SUCCESS OF THE BOLSHEVIK REVOLUTION IN 1917.

The focal point of the whole period 1903–24 is the second half of 1917, especially the night of 24/25 October. This was when the Bolsheviks seized power – by leading the trend of history, by imposing the trend, or by adapting themselves to where history seemed to be leading. These are the three main perspectives that have emerged over the subsequent eight decades.

The Soviet version

In October 1917 the political future belonged to the Bolsheviks. Their successors, the members of Communist regime, ensured that the roles of Lenin and the Party were fully acknowledged. According to the official Soviet version of what happened in 1917, the first aggressive blow was struck by the bourgeoisie, who seized from the proletariat the fruits of their revolution of February, 'determined to make short work not only of the Bolsheviks but of the Soviets as well'. It was the Bolsheviks who saved the proletariat and peasantry from renewed exploitation by overthrowing the bourgeois Provisional Government. The first stage in this process was to supplant the Socialist Revolutionaries and the Mensheviks as the main influences in the Petrograd Soviet: 'The Bolshevik Party had become the generally recognised leader of the revolutionary struggle of the proletariat and all the other working people.' The second stage was to select the most opportune moment for toppling the Provisional Government. This was the achievement of Lenin, who over-rode opposition from such traitors as Kamenev, Zinoviev and Trotsky which could have wrecked the whole process. 'The Bolshevik Party led by Lenin inspired and organised the October Revolution.' Indeed, Lenin's personal contribution cannot be overestimated. 'Lenin had studied the revolutions that had taken place in a number of countries and summed up the vast experience of insurrection gained by the proletariat and other working people.' The October Revolution was successful because of the participation of 'huge masses of people' and because 'Lenin chose a suitable time for it when the forces of the enemy were demoralised'. He was therefore able to bring 'a preponderance of strength' in the 'critical sector'.[1]

The basis of this interpretation is that the people were roused to action by a party and leader who showed them how to reclaim what was rightfully theirs. This accords with what the future regime wanted as the image of its origins. The reputation of the Bolshevik Party would be best preserved by projecting it as strong, in control and ready to act. On the other hand, there had to be a certain emphasis on its action as defensive, otherwise there might be a case for the Bolsheviks trying to overthrow the popular revolution of February. It would be more effective, in this case, to present the bourgeoisie as the aggressors and the Bolsheviks as taking swift defensive action through a bold strategy initiated by Lenin. This, too, had to be emphasised, since the Soviet state needed a eulogy on behalf of its founder. The official Soviet biography of Lenin therefore makes much of his 'genius as a leader of the masses' and his skills as 'a wise and fearless strategist'. Hence 'The leadership given by Lenin and the Bolshevik Party, the valiant struggle and heroism of the workers of the Red Guard, the soldiers and sailors, ensured the success of one of the greatest events in world history – the overthrow of the power of the landowners and capitalists.' There also had to be a new dawn, a new era that could be described only in superlatives. 'The victory of the Great October Socialist Revolution turned a new page in the history of mankind, ushered in the era of the downfall of imperialism and the triumph of socialism and communism.'[2]

The non-Soviet liberal view

The non-Soviet liberal view also lays emphasis on the strength of Bolshevik organisation and leadership. It does not, however, accept as a corollary the automatic connection between Bolshevik organisation and popular support. A key force behind the liberal perspective is outrage. The Soviet perspective is that in February the bourgeoisie grabbed the victory achieved by the proletariat; the liberal perspective is that in October the Bolsheviks seized power from the democrats. The starting point for this attitude is probably the explanation given in 1932 by Kerensky for his fate at the hands of the Bolsheviks: 'Only by way of conspiracy, only by way of treacherous armed struggle was it possible to break up the Provisional Government and stop the establishment of a democratic system in Russia after the Revolution.'[3] A substantial number of historians took up the theme of 'conspiracy' and 'treacherous armed struggle'; the Bolsheviks were efficient, well organised and led by a master strategist – but they had little genuine backing. Lenin made full use of the type of structure he had imposed upon the Party, a carefully controlled core of people engaged in revolution as a profession. With this he was able to take advantage of the other parties in Russia as they lapsed deeper into crisis during the course of 1917. The method showed flexibility and resilience; Lenin alternated judiciously between withdrawal and attack, depending on the strengths and weaknesses of the opponent. But the process was profoundly undemocratic as it did not represent the wishes of the majority of the population – the peasantry and a substantial part of the urban workforce. Instead of creating genuine popularity through widespread support, the Bolsheviks projected an illusion. Merle Fainsod, for example, wrote in 1953 that 'The party's role in directing the insurrection was camouflaged behind the façade of the Soviet. This shrewd stratagem provided a measure of pseudo-legality for the organizers of the insurrection.'[4]

This perspective is almost equivalent to Russian history being pushed up a cul-de-sac, until its mainstream direction could be rediscovered with the collapse of Communism in 1991. The underlying motive is sympathy with the attempts of the moderate parties to find a solution to Russia's long-standing problem of autocratic rule. They appeared to be moving towards a more open society and discovering the real measures of Western influence when the Bolsheviks closed down the experiment and reverted to authoritarianism in the name of a new and alien ideology. The Bolsheviks therefore cease to be heroes in any moral sense, although it remains possible to admire their persistence and success.

To an extent, all this is affected by a retrospective view of Russian history. This, in turn, was influenced by developments within the Soviet Union itself. In 1956 Nikita Khrushchev launched an attack on Stalin's leadership and provided evidence of the atrocities committed by his regime. This had no effect on Soviet historiography of Lenin, since he preceded the distortions of Communism that Khrushchev attributed to Stalinism. But it did have an impact on Western historians who, in a new awareness of just how vicious the Stalinist regime had been, were prepared to revisit the origins of this regime in the Bolshevik Revolution. Khrushchev's condemnation of Stalin further confirmed the liberal interpretation in its focus on the influence of key individuals. If Stalin had been so dominant after 1929, there was an even stronger case for Lenin's total primacy between 1917 and 1921. In other words Khrushchev unknowingly did much to prolong the Western emphasis on history operating from above.

The western revisionist view

But historiography, as well as history, moves on. There is now a strong revisionist alternative, although it comes in two distinct strands. First, the Bolsheviks were much more in tune with popular demands than was previously recognised. Second, their organisation was far less structured and effective. Recent historical studies, of other European countries as well as Russia, have fundamentally reconsidered the way in which political power operates. It is now argued that there has been too much emphasis on the idea of power being a process that is exercised downwards by leaders and organisations over the people. Instead, there needs to be more recognition that leaders and organisations can be influenced by pressures from below. The practical effect of the new perspective is that the Bolsheviks are now seen as being much more in line with the most immediate wishes of large parts of the population. Instead of forcing the pace of revolution by exploiting popular grievances, they were adapting their policies to enable them to move with a revolutionary current that already existed. The people therefore had a vital influence on events. Edward Acton's succinct summary of the revisionist view is that 'The driving force behind their intervention, their organisational activity and the shifts in their political allegiance was an essentially autonomous and rational pursuit of their own goals.'[5]

Which groups exerted the most influence on the Bolsheviks? One, which has in the past been greatly underestimated, was the peasantry. They provided a radical impetus, insisting on the transfer of ownership of the land to those who worked it and taking action to ensure that this happened. Peasant petitions also demanded justice through peasant courts, elected local authorities and more extensive education. Although there were frequent revolts, violence was not mindless but aimed at eliminating opposition to such designs. The Bolsheviks would have been unwise not to take note of such pressure. This explains the tactical adjustments to their policy made in the *April Theses* and subsequent pronouncements on land ownership, which were not exactly in line with Marxist collectivism. The urban workers also exerted pressure. The most active were the skilled workers, who tended to dominate the local soviets and factory committees. Like the peasants, they were radicalised by their own aspirations rather than by stimulus from the Bolsheviks. Elements within the army reacted in very much the same way. Their two main demands were the democratisation of the command and an early end to the war. This war weariness was less the result of external agitation, especially from the Bolsheviks, than from a deep welling up of discontent as a result of years of defeat and suffering. Rather than being manipulated, therefore, these groups pressurised the Bolsheviks into taking action on their behalf. The Bolsheviks succeeded because they followed rather than established the trend.

This reconsideration of the pattern of support has had implications for Bolshevik organisation. The Bolsheviks were not as well organised as had previously been thought; however, this did not matter since they were in a stronger position than their rivals, the Socialist Revolutionaries and the Mensheviks, who had sacrificed much of their credibility in 1917 by urging support for the policies of the Provisional Government. Instead of being highly centralised and conspiratorial, the Bolshevik Party was more democratic and decentralised. The essential point is that the Bolsheviks adapted to the goals of the various sectors of society rather than created these demands. Centralised structures would have been a liability in this process of adaptation. The coup itself was carried out by Trotsky and the Military Revolutionary Committee – in the name of the soviet. But this was not a façade or pretence at democracy. The soviet had genuine influence over the decisions taken by the Bolsheviks against the Provisional Government, although possibly not over the seizure of power itself. Irrespective of whether the soviet and the workers' committees approved of the seizure of power, they were certainly not likely to try to prevent it. This was because of the way in which they had swung behind the Bolsheviks during the course of 1917; the revolution was, after all, being carried out in their name.

Revisionist historians therefore argue that the Bolsheviks represented the general revolutionary trend in 1917 more effectively than any of the other revolutionary parties. In the light of this, efficient and conspiratorial revolutionary organisation, previously emphasised by liberal historians, did not particularly matter. This new approach may seem radical but there are reasons behind it. One is the extent of recent research into the details of trade union and peasant activities during 1917. Another is the emergence of a new methodology, a new style of interpretation, which pays as much attention to the influence of the population at large as to individual leaders. The new history from below therefore acts as a counterweight to the more traditional history from above. Third, crucial events in recent Russian history are bound to have had an effect on Russian historiography. Particularly important are the introduction of *glasnost* by Gorbachev in 1987 and the collapse of the Soviet Union at the end of 1991, both of which altered the perspective on Soviet history as a whole.

Summary

The Soviet and revisionist views both see the Bolsheviks as representing the interests of the population, although the Soviet argument is that the Bolsheviks interpreted and led these, while revisionists maintain that the Bolsheviks were basically opportunists, switching their policies to meet the people's expectations. Both differ from the liberal view, which is that the Bolsheviks had no real claim to popular support. On the issue of organisation there is more of a connection between the Soviet and liberal arguments: both maintain that the Bolsheviks were carefully organised and led. However, the Soviet view interprets this as enabling them to act on behalf of the popular majority, while the liberal approach claims that it made possible a minority Bolshevik conspiracy. Revisionists, by contrast, tend to present a case for the *lack* of effective Party organisation and structure.

The relationship between different styles of interpretation is usually dialectical. They influence each other and syntheses generally begin to emerge. Students of modern history should be able to follow several possible alternatives here.

Questions

1. Were the events of October 1917 a 'popular revolution' or a limited 'military coup'?
2. What motives would historians have for ascribing the terms 'popular revolution' and 'military coup' to the events of October 1917?

ANALYSIS (3): CONSIDER THE STRENGTHS AND WEAKNESSES OF THE DIFFERENT INTERPRETATIONS OF BOLSHEVIK SUCCESS IN 1917.

Each of the major waves of interpretation has positive and negative features, with some surprising twists of emphasis.

The Soviet interpretation

The Soviet interpretation is probably the most fundamentally flawed. The basic problem with any political approach to history is that history serves a purpose that is higher than academic explanation. What really matters in this case is that the reputation of the regime is built on secure foundations. History therefore overlaps ideology to produce an idealised version of events. Some of the interpretations are tenable. For example, the emphasis on Lenin's inspirational leadership and on the organisation provided by the Central Committee overlaps the slant of the liberal approach as an explanation for the success of the Bolshevik Revolution. The difference, of course, is in the Soviet conception of Bolshevik heroes guiding history through the Marxist dialectic against the liberal assumption that history can be pushed in any direction by individuals and groups who are sufficiently ruthless. A second example of a strand in the Soviet view that parallels another interpretation is that the Bolsheviks received widespread popular support. This is very much in line with the recent revisionist view. On the other hand, the revisionist corollary – that the support was attracted by the Bolsheviks temporarily shifting their policies to conform to pressure from below – remains out of joint with the Soviet ideal of Bolshevik guidance and leadership of public opinion. What weakens the overall Soviet approach is its rather tedious dismissal of any possible alternative. Propaganda is deducible as much by its style as by its content.

More specifically, there are major factual distortions in the Soviet version. One concerns the Kornilov Revolt of August 1917. The *Short History of the CPSU* argues that Kerensky and the Provisional Government 'were privy to this conspiracy' and that they appealed to the masses for help only when they realised that Kornilov 'would not only hang the Bolsheviks but would also shoot down the Socialist Revolutionaries and Mensheviks'. This implies an automatic connection between two enemies of the Bolsheviks and a dismissal of any possibility that they might have been enemies of each other. The analysis also distorts Trotsky's role. He is seen as a dead weight who 'very nearly wrecked the armed uprising' by disagreeing with Lenin over the timing.[6] This view has two weaknesses. First, it probably attributes too much influence to Lenin at the start of hostilities; even partial acceptance of the revisionist interpretation would indicate an upsurge of readiness from the soviet, which the Bolsheviks then rode into action. And, second, Trotsky was more directly connected to the popular sentiment by virtue of having been elected President of the soviet. The role of Trotsky in 1917 was almost certainly altered to fit the way he was later perceived to be an enemy of the Soviet state. It is a classic case of the present colonising – or Sovietising – the past.

The non-Soviet liberal approach

The liberal approach redresses some of the fundamental imbalances of the Soviet view. On the whole, it avoids political connections and polemicism, although it is free with criticism and judgement. Its main strength is the analysis of the origins of power, of the way it is concentrated and controlled, and of its impact on the lower levels of society. It also provides the best character studies of the individual leaders, especially Lenin, Trotsky and Kerensky. These are neither heroes nor villains; rather, they are individuals with strengths and flaws, who either control events or are overcome by them. The overall picture is more complex than that found in the Soviet version since there is a greater variety of personal motives and extraneous influences. Yet, at the same time, it is clear and sharp, creating an ordered view out of chaotic situations.

But the picture is perhaps *too* clear and sharp. Like the Soviet version, although for different reasons, it depends on a retrospective view. The solution to the problem of Bolshevik success and sudden emergence from relative obscurity is too neat; it invites the comment that it *must* have been more difficult than that. The essence of the liberal approach is to link eventual Bolshevik success with all the earlier stages of their organisation – and to relate both to the personal influence of Lenin. In fact, the Bolsheviks succeeded only at the very end of the process. Their achievements before autumn 1917 were quite limited, despite the extensive writings of Lenin on organisation and ideology. Although success may, as the liberal approach suggests, be due to earlier preparation, it can just as easily be the result of a sudden change of approach in the light of altered circumstances.

The revisionist approach

This brings us to the revisionist approach. Its strongest contribution is a new perspective on a wider variety of influences, with the mass of people influencing history to the same extent as individuals do. The result is a picture that is less sharp but which has greater depth. The Bolsheviks experienced eventual success despite, not because of, Lenin's earlier preparations and organisation. The circumstances of 1917 favoured opportunism and flexibility, not central organisation and fixed positions. Lenin did not lead from above; he was influenced from below. Revisionist history swells the stream of revolutionary activity so that the Bolsheviks become merely one of the channels: they achieved success only when they realised that they had to go with the flow rather than try to channel it. Peasants cease to be innately conservative and workers no longer look to political ideologies provided from above. Revolution in Russia becomes an elemental force that the Bolsheviks ride rather than lead.

Although it has performed a considerable service in enlarging the scope of history, revisionism still needs to come to terms with conflicting perspectives. Lenin and the Bolsheviks have been reassessed in one way but not yet in another. If they were able to attract such widespread support in 1917, they must have been profoundly antidemocratic in 1918 to have introduced the changes that drove such a large sector of the populace back to the Socialist Revolutionaries. And these changes need not necessarily have been due only to the exigencies of the Civil War. An obvious explanation would be that the Bolsheviks, Lenin in particular, were manipulative. This had been shown to positive effect in 1917 by attracting a wave of support through adapting their policies. It was shown to negative effect from 1918 by preventing an eddy of opposition by adapting their institutions. By this approach, revisionism begins to overlap with the liberal approach to Bolshevik ruthlessness – not in seizing power, but in *retaining* it.

The revisionist interpretation also has one area of more specific ambiguity. The Provisional Government, it is argued, fell because it had lost the confidence of the population at large. The Bolsheviks succeeded because they had the support of most groups at a time when the Mensheviks and Socialist Revolutionaries had become discredited. Yet early in 1918 the Bolsheviks found themselves confronted by many people who had reverted to supporting the SRs. This is explained by the sudden realisation that the Bolsheviks were establishing a dictatorship and effectively closing down the revolution. Logical enough so far, but there is still one problem. Much of the evidence for the popularity of the Bolsheviks comes from the factory, military or peasant committees, or from the Bolshevik majority in the Petrograd Soviet. But another source shows that the popular majority had turned against the Bolsheviks and reverted to their previous loyalties even before the Bolsheviks had begun to pursue an openly repressive policy. As soon as they had come to power the Bolsheviks arranged for an election of a new constituent assembly. Polling took place within weeks and the surprising result was that the Bolsheviks lost heavily to the Socialist Revolutionaries, winning 10 million votes (24 per cent of the total) to the SRs' 16 million (38 per cent). If the Bolsheviks were so successful in the second half of 1917 in reflecting public opinion, why did they not achieve a majority so soon after their successful seizure of power? Why, in particular, did they not experience a 'honeymoon period' with the electorate?

This may suggest that the momentum sweeping the Bolsheviks into power was not as strong as revisionist theories have assumed. In turn, therefore, there should perhaps be a partial return to acknowledging the importance of organisation and timing. Revisionism has the advantage of changing the sweep of interpretation but, in the process, is prone to overstate the alternative view. The history of historiography shows that the pendulum tends to return, although without prescribing a complete arc.

Questions

1. Which, in your view, is the strongest interpretation of the Bolshevik success in 1917?
2. 'It is possible to reconcile the official Soviet and Western

liberal interpretations of Bolshevik success in 1917. Neither, however, shares any common ground with the revisionist view.' Do you agree?

SOURCES

1. LENIN AND THE OCTOBER REVOLUTION

Source A: Extract from a letter from Lenin to the Central Committee of the Bolshevik Party, 24 October 1917.

Comrades, I am writing these lines on the evening of November 6th [24 October]. The situation is critical in the extreme. It is absolutely clear that to delay the insurrection now will inevitably be fatal.

I exhort my comrades with all my heart and strength to realize that everything now hangs by a thread, that we are being confronted by problems that cannot be solved by conferences or congresses (even Congresses of Soviets) but exclusively by the people, by the masses, by the struggle of the armed masses. We must at all costs, this very evening, this very night, arrest the Government. We must not wait! We may lose everything! History will not forgive revolutionaries for procrastinating when they can be victorious today (will certainly be victorious today), while they risk losing much, in fact, everything, tomorrow!

Source B: Extract from an official Soviet history of Lenin, published in 1959.

The Bolshevik Party, headed by Lenin, led the people of Russia to their great victory. The victory of October was the triumph of Leninism, a result of the hard, painstaking work, the heroic, intense struggle, which the Leninists carried on in the course of many years. It was a genuine revolution of the people.

Source C: Extract from Christopher Hill, *Lenin and the Russian Revolution*, published in 1947.

In pleading for haste Lenin was obsessed by two fears. The first was that the army command would open the front and surrender Petrograd, together with the Baltic fleet, to the Germans, as a lesser evil than surrendering it to the Soviet . . . Lenin's other fear was that the rising peasant revolt might get completely out of hand, and that when the Bolsheviks ultimately took over power, they might be faced with a situation of utter economic collapse and 'a wave of real anarchy may become stronger than we are'. This anxiety was, I believe, at the back of Lenin's mind from the day of his return to Russia, and that was one reason why the spinelessness and ineffectiveness of the Provisional Government enraged him so much: he feared that – as so often in nineteenth-century revolutions – it would play into the hands of a military dictator who would restore 'order'.

Source D: Extract from Robert Wolfson, *Years of Change*, published in 1978.

During the last weeks of October, plans for the coup were carefully made and 6–7 November [24/5 October] fixed as the date. On the evening of the 6th [24th], Lenin arrived at the party's headquarters, the Smolny Institute in Petrograd, to find everything carefully organized and ready. Early the next morning sailors on the battleship 'Aurora' opened fire on the Winter Palace across the river Neva. This was the signal for action. More than 20,000 troops were committed to the Bolsheviks. They now occupied the important strategic points of the city – stations, electrical power stations, main roads, the banks – almost without opposition. Only the Winter Palace remained untaken that day, guarded as it was by 100 cadet officers. During the night of 7–8 [25/6], Bolshevik troops moved up to surround it and got into the grounds. Early the next morning they moved in, again without a struggle and arrested the ministers of the Provisional Government, apart from Kerensky, who had already fled.

Questions

1. What does Source A reveal about Lenin's attitude to his colleagues in the Bolshevik Party Central Committee in October 1917? (5)
2. Use your own knowledge to explain the reference in Source C to 'the rising peasant revolt'. (3)
3. How far does a study of Sources B and D offer support to the view that October 1917 was a 'popular uprising'? (5)
4. Compare the value of Sources A and C to the historian studying Lenin's reasons for carrying out the October Revolution. (5)

*5. Using Sources A, C and D, and your own knowledge, would you agree that Lenin succeeded in winning power in October against overwhelming odds? (12)

Worked answer

*5. The Sources contain direct references both to the potentially dangerous position of the Bolsheviks and, at the same time, to the weakness of the Provisional Government. The Bolsheviks did face problems, but both the Sources and additional knowledge would suggest that 'overwhelming odds' would be an exaggeration.

Source A is the most directly related to the event. As such, it combines the advantage of immediacy and is a direct indication of how Lenin himself saw the situation. It shows extreme concern, as 'everything now hangs by a thread' and action was necessary 'at all costs' – otherwise 'We may lose everything!' On the other hand, two points suggest that the odds were not 'overwhelming'. One is that Lenin could count on the support of 'the masses' and the other that he was likely to have exaggerated the dangers in order to force the Party into action. Sources C and D have the advantage of longer-term perspectives and detailed historical research. As such, they can provide a retrospective analysis of Bolshevik action, although they are open to the individual slants of the authors' basic approaches (hence the phrase 'I believe' in Source C). Source C suggests that the obstacles were potential rather than actual – Lenin feared revolt by the army and the peasantry. Yet this was a spur to action, and the 'spinelessness and ineffectiveness of the Provisional Government' hardly constituted 'overwhelming odds'. Source D is quite dismissive of the problems confronting the Bolsheviks, stating that the key installations were occupied 'almost without opposition' and the ministers arrested 'again without a struggle'.

Additional knowledge tends to support the view that the Bolsheviks were not confronted by overwhelming odds. The weakness of the Provisional Government (referred to in Source C) had been brought about by the isolation of Kerensky and the collapse of his coalition after the attempted Kornilov coup in August. As the support for the Provisional Government sank, that for the Bolsheviks increased, so that by September they had achieved a majority in the Petrograd Soviet, while Trotsky had been elected its president. The Bolsheviks had also managed to win support from the peasantry, who were normally loyal to the Socialist Revolutionaries, as well as from the lower ranks in the army. Possibly, therefore, Lenin had less to fear from these areas than Source C suggests; the promises in his *April Theses* had made the masses impatient with the delay shown by the Provisional Government in introducing reforms. The Bolsheviks were well placed to seize power in October, especially in view of the effectiveness of their organisation, implied in Source D. This was due to the organisational strategy of Lenin, based on tight leadership and careful timing. This was one of the basic characteristics of the Bolshevik Party, going back to the 1903 Congress of the RSDLP.

2. DID THE REVOLUTION OF OCTOBER 1917 COME 'FROM ABOVE' OR 'FROM BELOW'?

Source E: Extract from *A Short History of the Communist Party of the Soviet Union*, officially approved by the Soviet Government (1970 edition).

The Bolshevik Party led by Lenin inspired and organised the October Revolution. Lenin had studied the revolutions that had taken place in a number of countries and summed up the vast experience of insurrection gained by the proletariat and other working people. He exposed the reformists who opposed the uprising . . . Lenin characterised the attitude of Marxists to an armed uprising and defined the conditions under which it was possible as follows: 'To be successful, insurrection must rely not upon conspiracy and not upon a party, but upon the advanced class. That is the first point. Insurrection must rely upon a *revolutionary upsurge of the people*. That is the second point. Insurrection must rely upon that *turning-point* in the history of the growing revolution when the activity of the advanced ranks of the people is at its height, and when the *vacillations* in the ranks of the enemy . . . are strongest. That is the third point.'

The situation in Russia on the eve of the October Revolution satisfied all these conditions. Since these conditions obtained it was necessary to approach insurrection as an art, i.e. to prepare for it thoroughly. Lenin demanded and demonstrated this art in his leadership of the uprising. He made sure that once the revolution got under way the Bolsheviks would see it through.

Source F: Extract from John Keep, 'Lenin as Tactician', published in 1968. At the time of publication the author was Reader in Russian Studies at the School of Slavonic and East European Studies at the University of London.

It must be emphasised that Lenin's ideas on tactics did not develop in a vacuum, but were a logical corollary of the 'organisational plan' which he outlined as early as 1902, and to which he adhered even when the scale of his operations was incomparably greater. Lenin was remarkably consistent. He seldom modified his ideas in the light of experience; on the contrary, as his self-confidence grew, he increasingly referred back to his earlier conduct as a guide to the problems of the present . . .

The first of these rules is that unswerving dedication to the final aim must be combined with extreme flexibility in the choice of means . . .

The second rule relates to the different techniques required in offence and defence. When conditions are favourable, the attack must be pressed home relentlessly . . . On the other hand, when the enemy is attacking, the correct tactic is to retreat in good order, regroup one's forces, and prepare for the inevitable turn of the tide . . .

From these directives it follows that no single mode of action can be considered valid in all circumstances, and that most situations demand a combination of several.

Source G: Extract from Alexander Rabinowitch, 'The October Revolution', published in 1997. At the time of publication, Rabinowitch was at Indiana University.

Tailoring the Bolshevik programme so that it would reflect popular aspirations was one of Lenin's most important contributions to the development of the revolution. However, contrary to traditional interpretations, in 1917 Lenin was not the all-powerful leader of a monolithic party . . .

Likewise, in 1917, Lenin's pre-revolutionary conception of the small, united, centralized party was discarded. Decision-making became more democratic and decentralized, the relatively free exchange of ideas was tolerated, if not encouraged, and tens of thousands of new members, whose aspirations helped shape policy, were welcomed into the party . . . The Bolsheviks' organizational flexibility, as well as their relative openness, and their extensive, carefully cultivated connections in factories, local workers' organizations, and military garrisons, were to be important sources of the party's strength.

Source H: Extract from Robert Service 'Lenin: Individual and Politics in the October Revolution', published 1994. At the time of publication, the author was Reader in Soviet History and Politics at the School of Slavonic and East European Studies, London.

And yet the challenge to the older conventional wisdom can be pressed too far. The notion that the October socialist revolution came wholly or nearly wholly from below is overstated. The revolution from above, initiated by Lenin in the Central Committee of mid-October and carried through on 25 October, still had a crucial impact. It was not the only impact, but it had vast importance nevertheless.

Questions

1. Which of Sources F to H do you consider to be least in disagreement with Source E? (15)

*2. Using Sources E to H and your own knowledge, consider whether in October 1917 Lenin introduced a full-scale 'revolution' or merely a limited 'coup'. (30)

Worked answer

**2. [Although all the Sources should be brought into the answer, this should be as evidence in the context of your own survey.]*

The range of Sources reflects a wide variation of views on whether Lenin led a 'coup' or a 'revolution' – or whether he led anything at all. This divergence is inevitable, given the controversial nature of the October Revolution, for reasons which are political or historical, polemical or academic.

Underlying the case for a full-scale 'revolution' is the original official Soviet view, reflected by the arguments in Source E and especially by the use of such sweeping phrases like 'a revolutionary upsurge of the people' and 'turning-point'. Lenin's role is seen as fundamental to the whole process both theoretically and in terms of his 'leadership'. Yet this approach has questionable validity as historical explanation. Its purpose is less to clarify the situation in October 1917 than to provide political justification for the regime that emerged from it. The subsequent Soviet regime needed a revolution and a founding leader – and both were bound to be idealised. The past, in other words, was recreated for the image of the present.

However, this does not mean that the arguments for Lenin's role and for full-scale revolution are entirely negated. Other schools of thought raise different arguments that acknowledge at least one of these – although for different reasons. For example, the 'liberal Western' approach downgrades the 'popular revolution' to a 'minority coup'; this, however, was carried out with ruthless and efficient leadership. Source F is a typical example of this, emphasising Lenin's 'organisational plan' developed 'as early as 1902' and pursued with great consistency. It could be argued, however, that this approach shares with the Soviet view an exaggerated sense of Lenin's efficiency and that it assumes too readily that what Lenin wrote he also practised – even if there is a fundamental difference of opinion over whether he achieved a majority revolution or a minority coup.

A different strategy altogether would be to reverse the 'Western liberal' process by downgrading the importance of Lenin but, at the same time, exchanging the idea of the 'coup' for that of the full 'revolution'. The 'western revisionist' approach, exemplified in Source G, has the advantage of a longer historical perspective and can take account of the collapse of the Soviet regime in 1991. This is bound to degrade the importance of the founder of that regime, even to the extent of denying that Lenin was 'the all-powerful leader of a monolithic party'.

At the same time, the immense amount of historical research conducted over the past twenty years into social and local developments has fostered a newer and fresher argument that power comes 'from below' as much as it does 'from above', a view that is pressed by Rabinowitch. This is more convincing than either of the two earlier approaches since it takes into account a wider variety of factors; it also exists outside the context of either the Soviet Union or the Cold War, which tended to colour the other two.

And yet revisionist views, especially in their earlier phases, may be overemphasised – not for polemical reasons but rather as an attempt to gain acceptance as a genuine alternative. There is, therefore, a place for the 'post-revisionist', who may well belong to yet another school. This is the case with the author of Source H, who seeks to reset the balance between Lenin and 'the October socialist revolution', in the process moving partly back towards the argument in Source E – but without the latter's political agenda or polemical approach. Probably the most convincing line therefore would by the revisionist emphasis on the 'popular revolution from below' but without removing Lenin altogether from the picture.

6

THE BOLSHEVIKS AND THE RUSSIAN CIVIL WAR, 1918–22

BACKGROUND

Although they had seized power from the Provisional Government in October 1917, the Bolsheviks were still in control of less than one-sixth of Russia at the beginning of 1918. They were challenged on all sides by a variety of opponents.

Their major ideological enemies were the counter-revolutionaries, or Whites. These advanced on Bolshevik Russia from three main directions, before eventually being driven back by the Red Army, formed by Trotsky. The first attacks, which came from the south, were initially led by Kornilov, Deniken and Alexeyev. When these were contained in 1918, the southern initiative passed to Wrangel. The eastern front, meanwhile, saw extensive engagements with Kolchak's troops, culminating in the capture of Omsk by the Bolsheviks in 1919. In the Baltic area Yudenitch made a lunge for Petrograd but was driven back from the outer suburbs by Red Army cavalry.

The Whites were assisted by foreign expeditionary forces, which landed at widely dispersed points on the periphery of Russia. Archangel and Murmansk saw the entry of British, French, Italian, Canadian and American troops. The French landed in the Crimea, further British contingents in the Caucasus, and Japanese and Americans in eastern Siberia via Vladisvostok. These forces were used to protect supply dumps and communications rather than to assist the Whites in battle, and most had been withdrawn by their governments by the end of 1919.

Other integral parts of the Russian Civil War were the involvement of non-Bolshevik revolutionary groups, known as the Greens, and a spate of separatist national uprisings. In 1918 several Socialist Revolutionary governments were established in opposition to the Bolsheviks, while the Ukraine and the states of the Caucasus tried to establish their independence. In 1920 and 1921 there was also a full-scale war between Soviet Russia and Poland.

The conflict as a whole involved many millions of casualties and, with the exeption of the nineteenth-century Chinese Taiping Rebellion, was the bloodiest civil war in history. By 1921 the Bolsheviks had managed to extend their control from the European heartland to the whole of Russia, although they were then faced with widespread uprisings from peasant-based armies, some with support from the Socialist Revolutionaries; these were not finally suppressed until the end of 1922.

ANALYSIS (1): WHY DID THE BOLSHEVIKS WIN THE RUSSIAN CIVIL WAR?

The Bolshevik regime, set up in October 1917, occupied less than one-sixth of the total area of Russia. It was outflanked to the east by Socialist Revolutionary regimes and surrounded by White military offensives. Yet this widespread opposition and apparently vulnerable position both worked in the favour of the Bolsheviks, making it possible for them to secure eventual victory. What made this certain was the effectiveness of their own diplomacy, organisation and military strategy. Although the Bolsheviks benefited from external or objective circumstances, they also made their own luck at crucial moments. It is rare for success to result without a combination of the two.

The first example of this relates to the disunity of the opposition. The Bolsheviks were indeed fortunate that in the first few months of the conflict the Socialist Revolutionaries were unable to convert their political popularity into swift military victory. But Lenin's diplomacy also ensured Bolshevik survival in this crucial period. He acted quickly to remove the German threat in March 1918 by signing the Treaty of Brest-Litovsk, withdrawing Russia from the First World War. This enabled the Bolsheviks to focus on the internal situation. In August 1918 he also concluded a trade agreement, by which the Bolshevik government was to pay six billion marks and provide the Germans with one-quarter of the oil production of Baku on the Caspian Sea. In return the Red Army was able to take its focus off the west, especially the Ukraine, and switch its forces eastwards to deal with the Socialist Revolutionaries.

Even then there could well have been a stalemate, as the Bolsheviks would have been hard pressed to overthrow the Socialist Revolutionary governments. But this was to be done for them in a series of military coups conducted later in 1918 by Kolchak and others. Lenin and Trotsky now had the opportunity to turn a struggle with fellow-revolutionaries into one against counter-revolutionaries, which they were much better equipped to win. They were also able to persuade some of the Greens to join with the Reds to deal with the common enemy. In this they took full advantage of the intervention of the foreign powers on behalf of the Whites, which most Socialist Revolutionaries and Mensheviks found offensive. By December 1918 the Bolshevik leaders had entered negotiations with other socialist parties, including the Socialist Revolutionaries, to sink their political differences until after the defeat of the Whites.

During the conflict that followed the Bolsheviks benefited greatly from the deficiencies of the Whites, who did much to destroy their bid for power. The Whites operated a very disjointed military campaign. They had no real political base and even the areas through which they campaigned were not usually controlled by White governments: more often they were under conflicting warlords or in the chaotic aftermath of disintegrating socialist governments. The Whites also lacked a common strategy and failed to co-ordinate the separate campaigns of Yudenitch, Kolchak, Deniken and Wrangel. They had no overall policy, no ideology, no programme – and no overall leader. Unsurprisingly, they entirely failed to appeal to the masses, particularly the peasantry, who between late 1918 and 1921 saw the Bolsheviks as the lesser of two evils, fearing that the Whites would restore the powerful landlords and reimpose former dues and obligations. Nor were the Whites greatly assisted by foreign intervention. Comparatively few Allied troops were sent to Russia and of these none participated in the battles. The emphasis for Western governments was very much on concluding the First World War. There was also something inherently unattractive about supporting groups of nationalist conservatives who lacked even the pretence of a programme of reform. This meant that each Western government was internally divided over whether to maintain the intervention after the end of 1918, and politicians such as Winston Churchill, who wanted to continue an anti-Bolshevik crusade, were very much in a minority. By 1920 Lloyd George's coalition government in London had decided to withdraw any remaining British forces – despite Churchill's pleas – while the French government had decided to switch to a more defensive anti-Bolshevik strategy by bolstering Poland.

This provided a considerable array of objective advantages for the Bolsheviks. On the other hand, they made full use of their luck and formed a contrast with the Whites in almost every respect. They exploited their control over all the internal lines of communication, and Trotsky was able to deal with emergencies as they occurred, switching Red troops from one front to another to defeat White attacks swiftly. The Bolsheviks made the most of their control of the industrial heartland that included Russia's major cities, industrial centres and a rail network, which radiated outwards from Moscow. Trotsky's reorganisation of the Red Army was also vital here. He was able to increase the number of regular troops available to the Bolsheviks from 550,000 to 5.5 million, enabling the Reds eventually to outnumber the Whites by ten to one. Finally, the Bolsheviks had a clear and systematic ideology and used their control over all forms of communication to put across an effective propaganda campaign based on posters and the use of 'agitprop' trains.

The third stage of the war from 1920 to 1922 consisted of a series of more localised threats to the Bolsheviks, who were fortunate that the Socialist Revolutionary political and ideological infrastructure had in the meantime broken down. This meant that there could be no concerted anti-Bolshevik effort based on an alternative revolutionary strategy, as had existed in 1918. The peasant armies may have been temporarily stiffened by the guerrilla warfare of peasant leaders such as Antonov, but they were not up to resisting permanently the Bolshevik forces that had just gained experience from putting down the White armies. In any case, Lenin made crucial economic concessions to try to isolate the insurgents from widespread peasant support. In 1921, for example, he ended food requisitioning and introduced the New Economic Policy. This meant that there was no longer a cause for which the peasantry needed to prolong their resistance.

Bolshevik survival was therefore guaranteed by a combination of objective circumstances and the advantage taken of these by pragmatic and astute leadership. It is time to collate these.

Summary

The Bolsheviks were threatened early in 1918 by internal pressures from other revolutionaries and continuing external threats from the Germans. Clearly, they could not hope to win a war on two fronts. Lenin therefore took advantage of Germany's desperate need to end the war in the east in order to attempt a breakthrough in the west. This allowed him to concentrate on the mounting internal threat – disengaging from the First World War in order to fight the Civil War. This was precisely at the time when White coups overthrew Socialist Revolutionary regimes, offering the Bolsheviks a clearly defined enemy rather than the previous left-wing competition for popular support. The Bolsheviks succeeded in winning over much of the support formerly going to the Socialist Revolutionaries and Mensheviks by generating ideological hatred of the Whites through effective propaganda. The Whites, meanwhile, failed to co-ordinate their military campaigns, thereby losing their initial advantage of completely surrounding the limited areas held by the Bolsheviks. By contrast, the Bolsheviks turned the disadvantage of being surrounded into the advantage of controlling the strategic heartland of Russia. They made maximum use of the railway network to switch troops to the different fronts as required, while Trotsky's recruiting methods ensured that the Red Army had an overwhelming numerical advantage. They were fortunate that the withdrawal of the interventionist powers accelerated the collapse of the Whites, but the Bolsheviks had already won decisive military victories. As for the last phase of the war, the Bolsheviks certainly benefited from the disunity and disarray of the peasant armies. Nevertheless, Lenin ensured eventual success by removing one of the main irritants – grain requisitioning – a typical example of the flexibility of Bolshevik policies at this stage.

Questions

1 Why did the Whites lose the Russian Civil War?
2. How important was effective leadership to the outcome of the Russian Civil War?

ANALYSIS (2): HOW AND WHY HAVE VIEWS CHANGED ON THE ORIGINS AND SCOPE OF THE RUSSIAN CIVIL WAR?

For a conflict that was so traumatic for the peoples of a huge area, the Russian Civil War has been given less attention by studies of Russia than it has perhaps deserved. However, this has begun to change as the full range of its issues and impact has been considered. This analysis therefore involves several areas. Although there is the usual array of sub-debates and different shades of political influence, it is possible for this topic to confine the basic approaches to two.

How have views changed?

When it comes to defining the scope of the Civil War, there is at least some common ground between the official Soviet view and more traditional Western views. It was, they both argue, primarily a struggle between Reds and Whites. The Reds were aiming to save the Bolshevik Revolution and to extend it to all parts of Russia, while the Whites sought to bring down the Bolshevik regime and, with the help of foreign powers, restore the previous system. The Civil War was therefore about saving the October Revolution against attempts at counter-revolution. From this, the significance of the conflict is clearly the mobilisation of revolutionary forces and the expansion of the energies released in October throughout the whole of Russia. The official Soviet view was that the Bolsheviks were seeing off the 'foreign interventionists and the whiteguards'[1] and that the issue was the preservation and expansion of newly won Communism against the forces of ideological reaction. The result was a revolutionary dictatorship. In Soviet eyes this was the phase of the 'dictatorship of the proletariat' as predicted in the Marxist dialectic; to Western historians it was the radical phase of the revolutionary cycle, with the usual accompaniment of terror and repression (discussed in further detail in Chapter 7).

There have been considerable changes to this view as a result of the work of such revisionist historians as Evan Mawdsley, Geoffrey Swain and Vladimir Brovkin. The revisionist approach is that there were *two* civil wars. One was the conflict between different strands of revolutionaries to control the revolution. The other was between one strand of revolution and the attempts made to overthrow it. The former, has been called the Red–Green, or the 'forgotten', Civil War,[2] the latter the Red–White Civil War. The Red–Green Civil War commenced with a struggle between the Bolsheviks and the Socialist Revolutionaries between the end of 1917 and the middle of 1918. This was interrupted by the war between the Reds and the Whites between 1918 and 1920, before recommencing, from 1920 to 1922, as another Red–Green conflict, this time between the Bolsheviks and a series of peasant armies. The significance of these cross-currents is that the Bolsheviks were fighting as much against other forms of revolution as against counter-revolution. As a result, the dictatorship they established was a reversal of the previous revolutionary trend and assumed many characteristics of counter-revolution.

The revisionist approach has produced the following analysis of the Russian Civil War. The Russian Revolution had not played itself out by October 1917. Revolutionary influences were widespread in

1918 and there were still different strands of appeal. The Civil War was therefore as much about who should control the revolution as it was about combating attempts to reverse it.

On one side were the Bolsheviks. They had seized control on 25 October 1917 by overthrowing the Provisional Government. The Civil War broke out initially because the Bolsheviks refused to share power with other revolutionaries. Lenin had seized power to prevent a broader coalition in October. He also rejected conciliatory proposals by the Right SRs, victors in the Constituent Assembly elections, to form a coalition and a joint institution that would combine the Constituent Assembly with the pattern of soviets preferred by the Bolsheviks. When Lenin dissolved the Constituent Assembly, the Right SRs and other moderate socialists such as the Mensheviks became convinced that the Bolsheviks were trying to move too quickly towards socialism. According to S. Smith, reason demanded that the masses needed to be 'sobered up' and that policies should return to the 'realm of the possible'. Indeed, the SRs tried to convince the workforce that 'the revitalization of the industrial economy hinged on the overthrow of Bolshevik rule and the reconvocation of the Constituent Assembly, because only the Constituent Assembly could put an end to civil war and reunify the country as a single economic unity.'[3]

Dissatisfaction with Bolshevism was not confined to Petrograd and Moscow. Early in 1918 the Yaroslavl soviets elected Menshevik majorities, while the Right SRs and Mensheviks scored similar successes in Riazan and Kursk. When the Bolsheviks dissolved the soviets in all three areas, the moderates prepared to hold their ground. Within weeks there was widespread resistance to the Bolsheviks in the whole Volga region, including Samara and Yaroslavl, and the SRs established a directorate at Ufa, which extended as far as the northern region around Archangel. These areas pursued policies that aimed to preserve the revolution as a broad stream but to prevent the control of this stream by any Bolshevik clique.

However, it was precisely these regions that saw the transition from the Red–Green to the Red–White Civil War. The links in the chain were a series of military coups conducted by ex-Tsarist officers. An attempt was made in September 1918 in Archangel, which failed, followed by another in Omsk in November, which brought down the Socialist Revolutionary administration. The new regime, under Admiral Kolchak, became the main focus of the westward offensive against the Bolsheviks. Other White thrusts developed from the Baltic, under Yudenitch and from the south under Deniken and Wrangel. Again, moderate socialist governments were the preliminary casualties. The overall effect was to transform the conflict from competing strands of revolution to a direct confrontation between revolution and counter-revolution.

This was given an additional dimension by the intervention of foreign powers on behalf of the Whites. This is an area that has always featured strongly in more traditional analyses. Britain, the United States, France, Italy and Japan aimed to keep Russia in the war against Germany and to restore a regime that would acknowledge the debts that Tsarist Russia had incurred from them during the process of industrialisation. There was also a strong fear of Communism. Each of these motives gave the Bolsheviks strong ammunition for a propaganda campaign in that they were able to represent themselves as the only true guardians of the revolution, resisting Tsarist militarism which was co-ordinated by foreign capitalist enemies. The task of Lenin and Trotsky had therefore been greatly simplified.

The Red–White Civil War was largely over by late 1920 – certainly in central Russia, the Volga area, the Urals and much of Siberia. But, the revisionist line continues, the Bolsheviks were now confronted with a second Red–Green Civil War, or another 'internal front of the civil war'.[4] There was extensive upheaval in thirty-six provinces and armed resistance broke out in the west around Vitebsk and Smolensk, in Ryazan' and Penza in the east, and Orel and Kursk in the south, as well as in the Ukraine and Siberia. By April 1921 there were 165 peasant armies in Russia, about 140 of which were connected with the SRs. The largest of all the rebellions took place in Tambov Province, under the leadership of Antonov.

What were the reasons for this much-ignored part of Civil War history? The Bolsheviks simply referred to outbreaks of hooliganism and banditry, but clearly this was too dismissive. A more likely reason was the re-emergence of the tension between different revolutionary strands, which had been temporarily subsumed into the Red–White conflict. Many of the rebels again demanded an end to one-party dictatorship and a renewal of democratic elections. One slogan of the peasant armies was 'Soviets without Communists'. Unrest was also the result of peasant fears of the food levy, grain requisitioning and early attempts at collective farming; another peasant slogan was 'Down with State Monopoly on Grain Trade'. Finally, the SRs tried to co-ordinate initially spontaneous uprisings into a second great effort to wrest control of the revolution from the Bolsheviks. In May 1920 the SR Central Committee established the Unions of Labouring Peasantry, the intention of which was to destroy the soviets through prolonged guerrilla warfare. Colonel Makhin, the SR who took charge of the co-ordination, believed, 'The strategy dictates the necessity to begin popular insurrection on as large an area as possible at the same time, best of all everywhere. The power of a simultaneous action everywhere is enormous. No government is capable of coping with it.'[5] As it turned out, the Bolsheviks were able to apply the resources and experience gained in overcoming the Whites to a second offensive against the Greens. This proved to be the most exhausting and costly of the three phases of the Civil War.

Why have views changed?

History involves a constant revisiting of the past. In the case of the Russian Civil War several motives are clearly involved in the conflict of opinion about the issues involved.

The oldest of these is the polemical factor. The Soviet view is clearly based on an ideological emphasis that will continue to inspire loyalty to the regime that emerged. In this case history was written by the victors for the purpose of justifying their victory. Hence everything was painted with broad brushstrokes. On one side were 'the Soviet people', comprising 'workers and peasants' and led by 'Lenin and the Party'. On the other were 'foreign interventionists' assisted by the 'whiteguards'. The emphasis was very much on the attempt by imperialism and capitalism to overthrow the first victory achieved by Communism; this was fundamentally an ideological conflict in which the interventionists were the main enemy. The whiteguards were those sections of the Russian population who had not been won over, but they were a threat only insofar as they could be used by the interventionists.

Such a view simply could not remain unchallenged, as it involves a distortion of many of the components of the Civil War. Western historians not subject to the political influences of the Soviet system would make much more of the internal origins of the Civil War, even if many of them agreed that the main focus was a Red–White war. Although a distinction should be made between Whites and interventionists, the latter were not the main impetus behind the struggle. Their involvement was not part of an international capitalist conspiracy but a more limited attempt to install a regime that would return Russia to the First World War and enable it to pay off some of the debts incurred by the Tsarist regime. Furthermore, intervention faded rapidly once these two more practical objectives no longer seemed appropriate.

More difficult to explain is why Western historians should have developed the recent distinction between the Red–White and Red–Green wars. Unlike the controversy referred to in the last two paragraphs, this one is not about polemics or propaganda. It is mainly the result of looking again and, in the process, allowing new perspectives to emerge.

As the Civil War was fought the length and breadth of Russia, it must have been unusually complex. The instinct of historians is to prioritise in order to explain. This has, in the past, meant identifying a core issue and a number of peripherals. This produced a Red–White conflict that was further complicated by internal unrest affecting other revolutionary groups and the nationalities. Another way to explain the conflict is to refer to two interconnected issues. These were the struggle for the future of the revolution between different strands of revolutionaries, and the struggle between the revolutionaries and the counter-revolutionaries. Suddenly the former no longer appear peripheral, while the latter are no longer the key issue. The facts are not arbitrarily changed but their reinterpretation leads to a new overall perspective.

Within the overall change comes a new look at individual components. There is one particular example of this. In the past the existence of Socialist Revolutionary governments and the beginnings of the White offensives had been seen as coincidental or lumped together as 'anti-Bolshevik'. Now they are seen in a different light. The Socialist Revolutionary administration at Ufa was a major threat in its own right to Bolshevik ascendancy, since it represented an alternative and popular revolutionary impetus that might have successfully challenged the Bolshevik regime. The White offensive against the Bolsheviks began as a military coup against the Socialist Revolutionaries. This raises the interesting interpretation that the Whites removed the stronger threat to the Bolsheviks, substituting a weaker one with which the Bolsheviks were better able to deal. Instead of having to fight against a rival from the left, the Bolsheviks could now emphasise the ideological danger from the right. This, in turn, has implications for the future regime and for the way in which that regime viewed the Civil War. Revisionism can therefore bring about a new understanding of the Soviet version.

It is unlikely that the last word has been said about the Russian Civil War. Further changes of emphasis are likely in the future. These could well emphasise still further the confusing nature of the components but in such a way as to ensure that the interpretation of this confusion has an underlying logic. Historians are like that.

Questions

1. Why have some historians concentrated on the Red–White war, while others have upgraded the importance of the Greens?
2. Has the significance of the Civil War changed as a result of revisionist interpretations?

SOURCES

1. WHY DID THE REDS WIN THE CIVIL WAR?

Source A: A Bolshevik poster identifying the main enemies in the Russian Civil War. (Courtesy the Novosti Photo Library.)

(translated as "Wealthy gang beats the workers and peasants")

Source B: A report from the US Commander-in-Chief in Siberia, General Graves.

At no time while I was in Siberia was there enough popular support behind Kolchak in eastern Siberia or the people supporting him to have lasted one month if all Allied supports had been removed . . .

Kolchak was suspected, not without reason, of Tsarist leanings. Certainly, he was entirely void of any bias in favour of democracy. He hated and in return was hated by the Social Revolutionaries, who at the time were far and away the largest political body in Siberia. From the first his regime was distrusted and detested by all but the military clique which created it . . .

But deepest and most ominous of all was the hostility of the common people, who received this new dictatorship with a mistrust and alarm which grew in intensity . . .

All the old vices of the Tsarist regime came back. Floggings and beatings once again became the basis of army organization. The officers gambled, drank and stole military supplies, whilst the men starved.

Source C: Extract from Christopher Hill, *Lenin and the Russian Revolution*, published in 1947.

But what were the internal factors making for the survival of the Bolshevik regime?

First and foremost was the support of the organized workers, which the Bolsheviks won in 1917, and never lost. But four out of five inhabitants in Russia were peasants; and in order to obtain food to keep the war machine going at all during these years the government had to adopt pretty rough measures with the peasantry. How was it that the Bolsheviks nevertheless managed to retain peasant support?

Lenin dealt with this point in December 1919, when he asked why Admiral Kolchak, supported by the all-powerful Entente, had not been able to maintain himself in Siberia, the least proletarian area of Russia, the area which in 1917 cast the fewest votes for the Bolsheviks and the most for the Socialist Revolutionaries.

Questions

1. Using Source A, and your own knowledge, explain briefly whom the Reds considered their main enemies in the Russian Civil War. (5)

*2. Using your own knowledge and the Sources, to what extent do Sources A and C add to the information given in Source B? (8)

3. Using Sources A, B and C, and your own knowledge, would you agree that Bolshevik victory in the Russian Civil War was

due to the 'overwhelming support given to them by the Russian people'? (12)

Worked answer

*2. Sources A and C do provide some additional information to Source B, although there appears to be less concurrence between A and B than between B and C.

Source A provides a broader perspective than Source B of the opposition to the Bolsheviks. Like Source B, it appears to identify the 'whiteguards' as the main co-ordinating force, as General Graves suggested in his description of Kolchak. Nevertheless, while Source B gives the impression that Kolchak was isolated, 'hated by the Social Revolutionaries' and subject to the 'hostility of the common people', Source A warns of the whiteguards' domestic support from the bandit peasantry as well as ex-Tsarist officials and the Church. As a propaganda poster this is biased and polemical, but it does show that the Bolsheviks considered that such White leaders as Kolchak represented a broader base of opposition than Graves thought.

Source C seems to concur more directly with Graves's assessment. Both refer to the animosity between Kolchak and the peasantry, especially the Socialist Revolutionaries. Yet Source C raises the issue of the 'rough measures' adopted by the Bolsheviks against the peasantry, an additional perspective to Source B's observation that 'All the old vices of the Tsarist regime came back'. Yet ultimately the two sources are making a similar point: that the atrocities committed by Kolchak did as much as anything else to alienate the population. What Source C adds is an admission by Lenin that the area held by Kolchak had not initially been pro-Bolshevik, even though it rejected Kolchak's policies.

2. WHAT WERE THE SIDES IN THE RUSSIAN CIVIL WAR?

Source D: Extract from the Komuch Programme, June 1918. The Komuch was the Committee of Constituent Assembly, composed mainly of Socialist Revolutionaries. After Lenin dissolved the Assembly in January 1918 the Komuch formed a breakaway government in Samara.

The Soviet regime is overthrown and Bolshevism suffered complete defeat on all the territory which is now subordinated to the Committee of Members of the All-Russian Constituent Assembly. Nevertheless, there are still not a few people who dream of a return of the Soviet regime. These persons, together with the dregs of the population, energetically stir up the workers and peasants against the new government, exploiting their inadequate knowledge and capacity for organisation. These agitators suggest to them that the workers will again be under the power of capital and that the peasants will be deprived of the land and subjected to the landlords.

The Committee, regarding such agitation as clearly provocative, states that there is absolutely no basis for it and, in order to put an end to such malicious inventions, makes the following general declaration:

1. The land has once and for all passed into the possession of the people and the Committee will not permit any attempts to return it to the landlords . . .

8. The rights of the trade unions, as defined by law, preserve their force until the legal provisions are revised. Representatives of the workers and of the employers must be invited to participate in the preparation for a re-examination of the laws about the protection of labour . . .

Source E: Extract from *A Short History of the Communist Party of the Soviet Union*, published under the direction of the Soviet government (1970 edition).

The struggle against the foreign imperialists and the whiteguards lasted for three years. It was an unprecedentedly grim struggle and caused the young Soviet state incalculable hardship. Time and again the Soviet Republic faced a critical situation . . . All the [interventionist] armies were directed and strengthened by the military command of the leading imperialist countries. The enemy controlled the country's richest regions – the Ukraine, the Caucasus and Siberia. The foreign press of those days reported that the Bolsheviks were on the verge of collapse. It was repeatedly reported that Soviet power had ceased to exist.

But Soviet power had been set up by the people themselves, and it could not be destroyed in the same way as a people cannot be destroyed. Lenin, head of the Soviet Government and Chairman of the Council of Labour and Defence, and the Party appealed to the people and the Army every time the situation grew menacing. Their appeal gave birth to new forces. The finest members of the Party and fresh detachments of workers and Komsomol [the Communist youth organisation] members were sent to the threatened sectors, and the enemy, already proclaiming victory, suffered defeat and took to his heels. Hungry and poorly shod, dressed and armed, the men of the Red Army – all of whom were workers and peasants – displayed unparalleled self-sacrifice and heroism.

The struggle of the Soviet people against the interventionists and whiteguards was facilitated by the revolutionary struggle of the international proletariat. In the capitalist countries the working people disrupted the supply of weapons to the whiteguards and the interventionists . . . By the close of 1920 all the crusades launched by the imperialists and their allies in Russia were routed ... This was a signal victory in defence of Soviet power, the independence of the Soviet state and of the conditions for peaceful socialist construction.

Source F: Extract from Robert Conquest, *Lenin*, published in 1972.

While the bulk of the working class remained, if not as enthusiastically pro-Bolshevik as before, at least largely anti-White, Lenin's policies in the countryside, and his surrender of Russian territory at Brest-Litovsk, had nevertheless ranged the regime against most of the political and social forces in the country ...

While millions had served in the First World War, the Civil War consisted of encounters between Red armies of several hundred thousand and rather better equipped and trained but considerably smaller White ones, supported peripherally and erratically by a minor degree of allied 'intervention'. Lenin's was basically a victory by a weak and widely hated group over an enemy even weaker, no less hated, and politically far less clear-headed or united. The divisions existing among the 'Whites' were ... partly inherent in the whole White situation – the officer class ... were virtually incapable of political collaboration in any genuine sense with the more or less legitimate representatives of the majority parties of the Constituent Assembly.

Source G: Extract from Geoffrey Swain, *The Origins of the Russian Civil War*, published in 1996. At the time of publication, the author was Principal Lecturer at the University of the West of England, Bristol.

The Russian Civil War was not just the war between the Reds and the Whites, Bolsheviks and generals, which is etched in the popular memory; indeed, this war did relatively little to shape the subsequent Soviet regime – although it did much to create its propaganda image. The Russian Civil War was also a Red versus Green civil war, a war between the Bolsheviks and their socialist opponents led by the pro-peasant Party of the Socialist Revolutionaries (SRs), which started in May 1918 and ended only in June 1922 when the leaders of that party were put on trial. It was this Red versus Green civil war which shaped the Soviet regime, by establishing at the heart of Bolshevik policy a deep-seated antagonism towards the peasantry, something epitomized within less than a decade by Stalin's policy of forced collectivization of agriculture.

For the years 1919–20 this Red versus Green civil war became hopelessly entangled with the White versus Red civil war and subsumed within it. As a result, most studies of the Russian Civil War have concentrated on the White versus Red struggle, a complex enough topic in its own right, and skated over the Red versus Green civil war, describing the fighting of summer 1918 in terms of preliminary skirmishes before the fighting proper started, and treating all fighting after 1920 as essentially a policing operation by the victorious Bolsheviks, rather than a continuation of the events of 1918. This book takes a different approach: when the fighting which took place between 1918 and 1922 is seen as a whole, the origins of both the White versus Red and Red versus Green civil wars have to be traced . . . Indeed, any study of the origins of the Russian Civil War inevitably leads to a more detailed analysis of the Red versus Green war which both preceded the Red versus White war and continued after it. A history of the origins of the Russian Civil War must be in essence the rediscovery of this forgotten civil war before the civil war.

Questions

*1. Analyse and explain the different interpretations in Sources D and E of (a) the main enemies of the people and (b) the measures taken to deal with them. (15)

2. Using Sources D to G, explain why historians have differed in their interpretations of what the Russian Civil War was about. (30)

Worked answer

*1. Sources D and E approach the issues of 'enemies of the people' and 'measures to deal with them' in different ways. This is hardly surprising since the two sources from which the extracts were taken were written for different purposes.

According to Source D, the main enemies were those 'who dream of a return to the Bolshevik regime', while Source E places the emphasis on 'foreign imperialists' and 'whiteguards'. The authors of the Komuch Programme blamed Lenin's regime for the collapse of the genuinely democratic forces of revolution and were determined to deal with the 'dregs of the population' attempting to reverse the 'complete defeat' suffered by Bolshevism. Source E, by contrast, avoids any reference to the conflict between different types of revolutionaries, concentrating instead on the counter-revolutionary threat of the whiteguards and the external danger posed by the 'capitalist countries'. The measures needed were directly related to the nature of the perceived threat. Since the Bolsheviks had to be prevented from recovering from their defeat in the Komuch-held area, Source D looked to guarantees of liberties already won; hence peasant ownership of land was to be retained and the rights of labour carefully defined and protected. Source E, on the other hand, emphasises the importance of military measures based on 'the men of the Red Army' who were able to rout 'the crusades launched by the imperialists and their allies in Russia'.

The different approaches can be attributed to the purposes of the two sources. As a programme guaranteeing the constitutional status of the Constituent Assembly, Source D was bound to emphasise that the main threat was Bolshevik, as they had closed the Assembly in January 1918 and substituted a system of Bolshevik-controlled Soviets. The issue was one of asserting democratic rights against the growth of Bolshevik dictatorship. Source E, however, was a polemical version of history designed to uphold the Soviet regime through a favourable interpretation of its origins. This explains the focus placed on more fundamental enemies who opposed the concept of revolution. An attack on the Komuch would only complicate the issue – and raise the potentially embarrassing issue of how the Komuch was able to establish itself in the first place. Source E therefore seems much more comfortable in converting the conflict into revolutionaries versus counter-revolutionaries, rather than regarding it as an internal battle between revolutionaries themselves.

7

THE BOLSHEVIK REGIME, 1918–24

BACKGROUND

Between the October Revolution in 1917 and the death of Lenin in January 1924, Russia went through a series of changes. Politically, it moved in the direction of dictatorship. The Constituent Assembly was dissolved in January 1918, ending the prospect of a parliamentary democracy. Instead, the political structure was based on the soviets, which were in turn dominated by the Bolshevik (later Communist) Party. Although two constitutions were drawn up in 1918 and 1922, these operated under the same constraint. The multi-party system was also destroyed in a period of terror (1918–22) under the agency of the secret police, the Cheka.

Economic change followed a more chaotic course. Early developments between October 1917 and the middle of 1918 were confined to confirming the peasantry in their ownership of the land and nationalising only a few key industries and enterprises. The pace was accelerated by War Communism, adopted between 1918 and 1921. This introduced grain requisitioning and more general nationalisation. It was, however, so fiercely opposed that the regime was forced to backtrack into the New Economic Policy in 1921. This was essentially a compromise, in which the regime settled – for the time being – for 'state capitalism'. It was not, however, accompanied by any political liberalisation.

Each of these developments was bound up with, and probably radicalised by, the Civil War (see Chapter 6).

ANALYSIS (1): HOW DID THE BOLSHEVIKS CHANGE RUSSIA'S POLITICAL AND ECONOMIC STRUCTURE BETWEEN OCTOBER 1917 AND 1924?

The Bolshevik Revolution of October 1917 swept away the Provisional Government and forced its members to flee the Winter Palace and Admiralty Buildings or face arrest. Apart from that, there were several examples of initial continuity. The Congress of Soviets remained in existence and the Bolsheviks soon carried out the pledge of the Provisional Government to organise elections to a new constituent assembly. The various political parties – Cadets, Socialist Revolutionaries and Mensheviks – also retained their separate identities, even if the Left SRs and Menshevik Internationalists had thrown in their lot with the Bolsheviks. Major decisions had still to be taken and there was widespread expectation of a new era of broad revolutionary consensus.

The economy was similarly unaffected by immediate change. The only measure introduced in the wake of the October Revolution was the Decree on Land, which confirmed the peasant takeover of the nobles' estates, without, however, introducing large-scale socialist collective production. Similarly, the Decree on Workers' Control gave workers a share in the control of the management of industry. There was, however, no immediate attempt at widespread nationalisation to bring industry under state control. If Lenin did intend to create an economy based on Marxist principles, he showed no desire at the end of 1917 to rush into it.

By 1924 the situation had changed – but not entirely. The Bolsheviks had introduced a very different political structure and had also attempted to transform the economic base. They had been forced into retreat on the economic front but, at the same time, managed to maintain a firm grip on the institutions of political power.

Political change

During the course of 1917 the Bolsheviks transformed Russia from an incipient parliamentary democracy with an array of parties into a single-party dictatorship with a monolithic ideological base.

The first casualty was the Western-type Constituent Assembly. The elections of November 1917 produced a sweeping majority for the

Socialist Revolutionaries over the Bolsheviks. In January 1918 Lenin therefore dissolved the Assembly and put an end to the hopes of the other socialist parties that a Western democracy would emerge. This was clearly a pragmatic response to popular pressures that threatened to unseat the Bolsheviks, but Lenin justified it by a new layer of ideology. He explained that the Assembly was 'an expression of the old relation of political forces'.[1] He now confirmed that 'a republic of soviets is a higher form of democratic principle than the customary bourgeois republic with its Constituent Assembly'.[2] This was directly opposed to the policy of the Menshevik leaders, who saw the soviets as means of expressing popular opinion only in exceptional times; after the end of the crisis, they argued, the soviets would take second place to the more conventional institutions of democracy. But Lenin's priority was to close down, to all but the Bolsheviks, access to the revolution and the power it had generated. This meant that the powers of the soviets had to be carefully controlled. Hence, although their number increased rapidly from 1918, their influence declined steadily.

The hand that controlled these instruments was the Bolshevik Party, shortly to be renamed the Communist Party. This was brought under renewed discipline, all power leading upwards to the Central Committee. This, in turn, had three specialised organs in the form of the Politburo, Orgburo and Secretariat. The Party dominated the soviets at all levels to ensure that Socialist Revolutionaries and Mensheviks were denied access. Indeed, according to a Party resolution of March 1919, 'the strictest centralism and the most severe discipline are an absolute necessity'.[3] The process was described as 'democratic', but not in a western or bourgeois sense. Instead, Lenin's term 'democratic centralism' came to epitomise the complete subordination of state organs to the Party – the main characteristic of the Communist regime within Russia between 1918 and 1991.

These changes were carried out by force. Both Lenin and Trotsky believed in the need for terror, although this was to be justified in 'the name of the interest of the workers'.[4] Between December 1917 and February 1922 the secret police, the Cheka, hunted down opponents of the regime and, by one calculation, executed over 140,000 people. This may be compared with a total of 14,000 dispatched by the Tsarist secret police, the Okhrana, under the last two tsars. Trotsky, a hardliner on the use of terror, explained the strategy on the grounds that 'we shall not enter into the kingdom of socialism in white gloves on a polished floor'.[5] The first group to be dealt with by the Cheka were the anarchists, their views of unfettered political liberty being seen as a threat to the Bolshevik theory of the dictatorship of the proletariat. The moderate socialists

– Mensheviks and Socialist Revolutionaries – were expelled from the soviets during the course of 1918, while thirty-four Socialist Revolutionary leaders were put on public trial in 1922. There is a strong suspicion that terror was more about eliminating other revolutionaries than it was about preserving the revolution.

Yet the emergence of the one-party state was not a guarantee against dissent and unrest. If anything, the Bolsheviks encountered more extensive opposition as a result of their actions against the other parties. The critical year was 1921, when the Cheka reported no fewer than 118 separate uprisings. One example was the Kronstadt Revolt, which carried demands for soviets without Communists, elections by secret ballot and an end to the belief that the only alternative to a bourgeois regime was the dictatorship of the Communist Party. Although the Kronstadt Revolt was suppressed by Trotsky and Tukhachevskii, the threat was taken seriously by Lenin, who referred to it as 'the biggest . . . internal crisis' of the period. Since the immediate cause had been the appalling economic situation, Lenin's response was to moderate Bolshevik economic policy, while, at the same time, maintaining his grasp on political power by ensuring that the opposition parties did not re-emerge. He proceeded therefore by trial and error rather than by systematic policy. Only when he was fully satisfied about the security of the Bolshevik position did he end the terror by closing down the Cheka in February 1922.

Other potential threats to Bolshevik control were the aspirations of the various nationalities. Tsarist Russia had contained many captive peoples who had seized the opportunity provided by the First World War and the Bolshevik Revolution to go their own ways. Some, like the Poles, Finns and Baltic peoples, achieved complete independence as a result of Russian defeat in the First World War. Others, like the Ukrainians and Georgians, stayed out during the Civil War but were brought back into line after the Bolshevik victories over the Whites. Lenin's approach to the nationalities was cautious and pragmatic. Originally he had viewed any form of federation with suspicion. Faced with the practical problems of the period 1918–24, however, he came to the conclusion that the only safe means of allowing for self-determination was through federalism. As a result, the constitutions of 1918 and 1922 established the two largest federations in the world: the Russian Soviet Federated Socialist Republic and the Union of Soviet Socialist Republics. This, however, was only a partial concession, for the total subordination of the organs of each republic to those of the Party ensured that federalism did not mean decentralisation. The USSR, in other words, was controlled by the Communist Party, and national self-determination was cancelled out by 'democratic centralism'. These constraints continued until the collapse of the Soviet Union in 1991.

Economic change

Theoretical Marxism demanded economic as well as political change. Any society, Marx and Engels had argued, consisted of a foundation – or base – and a superstructure. The former comprised the economic system upon which the society was constructed, the latter the political and social institutions that were created by the foundation. A change of institutions therefore needed to be accompanied by a transformation of the economy. Lenin probably intended to transform the Russian economy by wiping out all 'exploitation of man by man' and eliminating the division of society into classes by means of a temporary 'dictatorship of the proletariat'. But he found that his hands were tied, first by the need to adjust Bolshevik policies in 1917 to popular demands and, second, by the rapidly changing circumstances between 1918 and 1924. The result was anything but the planned system that Marxism predicated. Rather, it was characterised by trial and error.

As we have seen, in the first step forward, taken between November 1917 and mid-1918, the emphasis was on caution, and nationalisation was applied only to banks, foreign trade and armaments works. In particular, Lenin was careful to avoid antagonising the peasantry and made every effort to win them away from the party they had traditionally supported – the Socialist Revolutionaries. Hence, by the middle of 1918, there had been no attempt to introduce collective ownership in agriculture, while the only enterprises brought under government control were banks, certain forms of trade and armaments works.

Then, in mid-1918, came a major change, with the introduction of a policy generally known as War Communism. This was basically an attempt to replace the free market by state control over all means of production and distribution. The Decree on Nationalisation, for example, covered all large-scale enterprises, while grain requisitioning greatly reduced the food stocks of the peasantry in order to supply the workers in the cities and the troops fighting the Whites. The result was chaos. The monetary economy disintegrated, to be replaced by barter and black-marketeering. This was not helped by the policy of the government forcing up inflation by printing notes to obtain essential supplies. Grain requisitioning led directly to a drastic decline in production as the peasantry lost all incentive to labour, with the result that there was a shortage of food in the cities. War Communism could be enforced only by the use of terror on an unprecedented scale; the peasantry suffered particularly severely as their grain supplies were forcibly removed by Cheka detachments. Not surprisingly, there were widespread peasant rebellions that prolonged the Civil War into a 'second Green phase' (see Chapter 6), along with strikes and riots that shook the very foundations of the Bolshevik regime.

So, in 1921, there was a strategic withdrawal. The basic strategy was now to restore to the economy a degree of capitalism and private enterprise. Introducing his New Economic Policy (NEP), Lenin argued that the road to socialism would be longer than originally thought. 'Our poverty and ruin are so great that we cannot at one stroke restore full-scale factory, state, socialist production.'[6] It was also impossible to think only in ideological terms: 'If certain communists were inclined to think it possible in three years to transform the whole economic foundation, to change the very roots of agriculture, they were certainly dreamers'.[7] Thus the peasantry were now permitted to dispose of their surplus produce on payment of a tax, and 91 per cent of industrial enterprises were returned to private ownership or trusts. The early results of the NEP were disappointing, as economic recovery was held up by famine (1921–2) and a financial crisis (1923). But, by 1924, the year of Lenin's death, considerable progress had been made, and by 1926 the economy had regained 1913 production levels.

Conclusion

Lenin's political and economic changes settled everything – and nothing. He set up political institutions that guaranteed that there would no longer be a threat to the Communist system; but he did not guarantee a political succession that would use the institutions with moderation. He arrived at a compromise between conflicting economic forces; but he provided no future strategy for this compromise to develop and grow. Hence the future of the regime became entangled with the future of the economy, resulting in even more extensive changes to both under the leadership of Stalin.

Questions

1. How complete was the dictatorship established by the Bolsheviks between 1918 and 1924?
2. 'Bolshevik economic policy between 1918 and 1924 was a failure.' Do you agree?

ANALYSIS (2): WHAT OPPOSITION EMERGED TO BOLSHEVIK RULE BETWEEN 1918 AND 1924? HOW DID THE BOLSHEVIKS DEAL WITH IT?

Any change of regime as fundamental as that which occurred in Russia in 1917 was bound to incur a wide range of opposition groups. The Bolsheviks may have represented at least a degree of public support in bringing about revolution in October 1917, but they provoked equal hostility when they took it upon themselves to interpret the future will of the public by establishing a dictatorship in 1918.

The more ideological types of opposition were predictable. There were still within Russia substantial sections of the population who were anti-revolutionary. Some were still supporters of the deposed Tsar and part of the White campaign was to bring about a royalist restoration. The Bolsheviks, however, forestalled this by killing the entire royal family at Ekaterinburg in 1918. Others were constitutionalists, who hoped that the October Revolution could be converted into a moderate, Western-type regime. The Cadets, for example, saw the future in a more secure and permanent form of the Provisional Government, without, of course, the influence of a Kerensky figure. But the Cadets were divided over how to achieve this. Some supported the Socialist Revolutionaries in their defiance of the Bolsheviks; others campaigned with the Whites in an attempt to eradicate all revolutionaries. The rest tried to keep their heads down, only to find themselves among the main targets of the Cheka after 1920. Within two years of the revolution all the counter-revolutionaries, whether reactionary or liberal, had been reduced to cartoon caricatures on Bolshevik posters.

More fundamental, and ultimately more damaging, was the opposition to Bolshevik rule that came from *within* revolutionary Russia – and from those who had a common antipathy towards both the Tsarist regime and the Provisional Government that had followed it.

The other revolutionary groups

The first signs of opposition from the other revolutionary parties emerged almost immediately after the October uprising. By far the largest of these groups were the Socialist Revolutionaries, established as a party in 1900. They had been undermined by their association with the Provisional Government in 1917 and by the defection of the Left SRs to an alliance with the Bolsheviks. Even so, they had hopes of sharing in government after the October Revolution; after all, they won 16 million votes in the elections to the Constituent Assembly, compared with the Bolsheviks'

10 million. When Lenin closed the Assembly in January 1918 the majority within the party, or Right SRs, understandably denied the legitimacy of the Bolshevik regime. The basis of its opposition was the Komuch Programme, which was intended to revive the Constituent Assembly and to give the future of the revolution back to *all* revolutionary groups. There was little chance of successful resistance in Petrograd since the Right SRs had already supported a failed counter-coup there on 29 October 1917. They could, however, retreat to their power bases and establish alternative governments. The most important of these was the Ufa Directorate, which, for a few months in 1918, became a rival to the Bolshevik regime. It was also a major threat since it could well have gone on to attract support from most of the rest of Russia. On this occasion the Bolsheviks were extremely fortunate; the Directorate was overthrown by a White military coup led by Kolchak, and in the ensuing chaos, the SR resistance to the Bolsheviks broke into three factions. One joined the Reds against the Whites, one the Whites against the Reds, and the third opted for neutrality between the two. This fracture destroyed the only future chance the SRs had to resist the Bolshevik regime. In 1920 and 1921 Russia was in the grip of widespread peasant uprisings. The Socialist Revolutionaries were again divided in their response and offered little practical help or political leadership. If they hoped to prolong their existence by continued neutrality, they were to be sadly disappointed. Once the Civil War and the emergency were over, Socialist Revolutionaries of all hues were hunted down, tried and imprisoned.

The other revolutionary group opposing the regime were the Mensheviks, part of the original RSDLP that had long criticised the authoritarian nature of Lenin's leadership. In 1917, however, they had split over whether co-operation with the Bolsheviks should now be renewed, with the Menshevik Internationalists opting for a broad coalition with them. Then, for a brief period in 1918, the Mensheviks reunited in their opposition to the Bolsheviks. The reason for this was the rapid drift of the new regime into dictatorship, the specific objection of the Mensheviks focusing on the dissolution of the Constituent Assembly in January 1918. But then another split occurred, which doomed the Mensheviks to ultimate extinction. The right of the party supported the campaign of the Komuch, set up by the Socialist Revolutionaries, while the left, under Martov, refused to take up arms against the Bolsheviks. Once the White invasions had started, the left-wing Mensheviks threw in their lot with the Bolsheviks and were given a degree of recognition by them until 1920. The rest went underground in the hope of joining a post-Bolshevik regime. From 1920 the entire Menshevik structure was doomed: its members were subject to the attentions of the Cheka, thrown into prison or, like Martov, forced into exile. By 1922 Menshevism had been virtually eradicated. It is not hard to see why. Having always preferred moderation and consensus, the Mensheviks were never in a position to exert serious challenge to their rivals, the Bolsheviks, who had been hardened by a tougher route.

Meanwhile, a third revolutionary group had emerged in opposition to Bolshevik policies – this time from within the Bolshevik Party itself. During the second half of 1918 Lenin had greatly extended the popular appeal of the Bolsheviks by adjusting the Party programme to meet popular demand. This meant, for example, a pragmatic acceptance of an early peace and of the private ownership of land by the peasantry. A number of left-wing Bolsheviks saw these policies as the betrayal of fundamental Communist principles. Withdrawal from the war by the Treaty of Brest-Litovsk (March 1918) was strongly opposed by some of the Party's intelligentsia (for example, Preobrazhenskii and Radek) on the grounds that it meant abandoning the aspiration to export the workers' revolution to the rest of Europe. Left-wing Bolsheviks opposed other, similarly pragmatic, policies followed by the Bolsheviks once the regime had become established. Particularly open to criticism was Lenin's economic compromise in the form of 'state capitalism' and the reliance on the Central Committee of the Party to run the new administration. Private ownership of the land by the peasantry was also criticised as playing into the hands of reactionaries. Such arguments however, were dealt with by a Communist Party that was becoming steadily stronger and more co-ordinated. Some of the critics were silenced by loss of membership, others by open defeat in Party Congresses. Above all, the dire emergency of the period 1918–22 enabled the Party leadership to present a powerful argument for special measures like 'state capitalism' and the NEP, which, as they themselves admitted, would not necessarily be permanent.

Popular opposition

One of the most striking features of the period was the level of popular opposition to the Bolsheviks. This applied in both the cities and the rural areas. The crucial date in both cases was 1921, when the Bolshevik regime came as close as it ever would to political collapse before 1991.

Urban opposition was largely spontaneous; that is, it was not connected with the revolutionary parties, whether Menshevik or Socialist Revolutionary, nor with the left-wing Bolsheviks. Instead, it developed as an outcry against Trotsky's labour conscription, food shortages, and the growth of dictatorship in government. Dissatisfaction was also widespread at the Kronstadt naval base, where demands were made for political reform, the key component of which was 'Soviets without Communists'. In the rural areas the main opposition was from Green armies, created from peasants disillusioned by the policy of War Communism and the forcible requisitioning of grain. The sheer scale was formidable: the Red Army had to deal with well over a hundred uprisings that, between them, imposed more demands than had the White armies in the earlier phase of the Civil War. No wonder Lenin later admitted that the crisis of 1921 was the worst the Bolsheviks had ever faced.

Yet the crisis was dealt with and the threat collapsed. There were three main reasons for this. The first was that the forces challenging the Bolsheviks had no overall co-ordination. The urban-based opposition based its hopes on reformed soviets, while the peasants insisted on a reconvened Constituent Assembly. And, even though the Socialist Revolutionaries had the same hope as the peasants, they made no concerted attempt to provide political leadership for their military action. Exhausting and enervating though it was, the Bolshevik counter-attack was bound to win in these circumstances. The second factor was therefore the discipline of the special forces of the Cheka, who advanced across the ice to overcome the Kronstadt Revolt, and the contingents of the Red Army who gradually ground down the peasants. Third, while these actions were being taken, Lenin was sufficiently pragmatic to realise that the military offensive had to be accompanied by a tactical retreat in terms of policy. This was carried out in the form of the NEP, which removed from the peasantry their most important motive for resistance.

The nationalities

Last, but not least, the various nationalities played a vital role in challenging the legitimacy of the Bolshevik regime between 1918 and 1922. Although Lenin had shown more sympathy than the other revolutionary leaders with the cause of national self-determination, the nationalities had always assumed that this was less than genuine. Hence, during the Civil War, several former provinces of the Russian Empire took advantage of the German-dictated peace of Brest-Litovsk to declare themselves fully independent. Lenin was forced to let go of Finland, the Baltic States and Poland. But he drew the line at the Ukraine and the states of the Caucasus. The logic of these states however, was, inescapable. How could they trust the goodwill towards national self-determination of a regime that had an ideological dislike of nationalism itself? Why, therefore, should Ukrainians and Georgians aspire to less than Finns and Poles?

The suppression of this nationalism was dictated by the result of the Civil War. Once the Bolsheviks had managed to defeat the White armies of Kolchak, Deniken and Wrangel, they were able to confront the peripheral dangers of the nationalities as well as the integral threats of the socialist groups. Hence the Ukraine was brought back into the Russian state as a result of the war with Poland (1920–1), soon to be followed by Azerbaijan, Armenia and Georgia. The remaining problems were taken care of by the characteristic Bolshevik combination of carrot and stick – coercion by the Cheka and the offer of a federal constitution. The former wiped out the nationality-based parties, while the latter offered the theory of a national self-determination based on the Union of Soviet Socialist Republics, set up by the 1922 constitution. In reality, however, this posed little threat to Bolshevik control since the federal system of the USSR was counterbalanced by the unitary structure of control by the CPSU, which was based on the Central Committee in Moscow.

Concusion

The survival of the Bolsheviks was accomplished by the destruction of the other groups that claimed with them an equal legitimacy and the right to an equal share in the government of the revolutionary regime. The Bolsheviks denied this legitimacy and their victory in the Civil War generated a momentum that could not be resisted – especially by opponents who were internally divided and inherently less ruthless.

Questions

1. Why were the Bolsheviks able to eliminate the Mensheviks and the Socialist Revolutionaries by 1924?
2. How unpopular were the Bolsheviks between 1918 and 1924?

ANALYSIS (3): EXPLAIN AND COMMENT ON THE DIFFERENT INTERPRETATIONS MADE BY HISTORIANS REGARDING THE INTERNAL CHANGES MADE IN RUSSIA BY THE BOLSHEVIK REGIME BETWEEN 1918 AND 1924.

One of the main themes of this book is the challenge to the establishment by revolutionaries. Another is its corollary: the conversion of revolution into the establishment. In this particular case, Lenin ceased to challenge one regime after 25 October 1917 and was involved in the process of establishing and defending another until his death in 1924. This had profound political and economic consequences.

Political change

Among the extensive historical debates covering this period is the theme of whether Lenin and the Bolshevik Party changed in their transition from revolutionaries to upholders of a regime – and whether they succeeded in the process. One view is that there was an underlying consistency between the Bolsheviks as revolutionaries and the Bolsheviks as the new rulers. This, of course, can be interpreted in a positive or a negative way.

The most positive of all is the official Soviet interpretation. The Bolsheviks had, in October 1917, seized power from the bourgeois Provisional Government, which had, in turn, stolen the fruits of the people's victory in March. 'From a Party devoted to the overthrow of the old system it became a Party dedicated to building a new society without exploiters, without oppression of man by man.'[8] This meant a major alteration in political relationships and institutions. But the impetus was dictated not by the Bolsheviks, who gave other parties a chance to share power, but by the 'petty-bourgeois' groups who resisted power-sharing. Hence the fate of the Constituent Assembly was decided not by the Bolsheviks but by the Mensheviks and Socialist Revolutionaries, who refused to acknowledge the overall supremacy of the Congress of Soviets and turned the Assembly into a centre of resistance to reform. Lenin therefore had no choice but to dissolve the Assembly and to confirm that the new system was to be based permanently on the soviets rather than on a bourgeois model. The 1918 constitution enshrined this principle, establishing a 'people's democracy'.

There was a similar sense of inevitability about the disappearance of the other parties, leaving the Communist Party as the only official form of popular representation. According to the Soviet interpretation, they 'gradually disintegrated and died a natural death in the course of a fierce struggle'. This was because, during the Civil War, 'the Menshevik, Socialist Revolutionary and other "petty-bourgeois" parties that had opposed the October Revolution found themselves in the camp of the enemies of Soviet power along with the parties of the bourgeoisie and the landowners'. Because they 'sided with the whiteguards and the interventionists', the Mensheviks and Socialist Revolutionaries 'were thrown on the rubbish heap of history'.[9]

The Soviet interpretation therefore makes the end of Russia's parliamentary experiment and multi-party system appear to be a progressive change, very much in line with their earlier ideals. Yet this is oversimplistic and leaves out a great deal. There is no mention of the use of terror by the Cheka. At the time, Trotsky justified this on the grounds that 'we shall not enter the kingdom of socialism in white gloves on a polished floor'. However, this theme is ignored in the 1970 edition of the *Short History of the CPSU*, for two reasons. One is that Trotsky had long since been discredited; the other was a desire to lift from the Soviet regime the stigma of the Stalinist terror and to rewrite history. In addition to ignoring the existence of Stalin and *his* secret police, the NKVD, the authorised version demanded the removal of any reference to the activities of the Cheka and its leader Dzerzhinsky. The result is a sanitised version of early Soviet history showing a people united in their enthusiasm for a democratic system created by the Bolsheviks. Fear had no place there.

There is, of course, another way of seeing the continuity in Bolshevik objectives and methods through 1917 and into 1918. The traditional Western view is that nothing changed significantly between October 1917 and 1924. The Bolsheviks came to power in a minority coup and then proceeded to impose a minority political dictatorship based on the systematic elimination of opposition through the deliberate use of terror to an unprecedented extent. John Keep, for example, emphasises the continuing priority given to power: Lenin 'conceived of the soviets as instruments of rule rather than sovereign bodies'.[10] The same applies to the use of coercion, which Lenin fully backed. We should not be surprised at the extent of Bolshevik repression or at the scale of the terror imposed. After all, the autocratic nature of the revolutionary Party had always discouraged democratic debate, while its efficient organisation and structure had made it easier to remove internal opposition. Why should the same principles not apply, on a vastly increased scale, when the Party had been transformed into a regime – especially when one of the bloodiest civil wars in history acted as a catalyst?

As with the Soviet interpretation, however, we can detect at least some retrospective interpretation. How much of the condemnation of Lenin's regime is due to the search for the roots of Stalinism? In turn, to what extent was the motive to condemn a system that was not only alien to the West but was regarded in the 1950s and 1960s as an ideological enemy to liberal democracy?

This invites a different perspective. Perhaps the Bolsheviks had good intentions, which they did not deliver when they came to power. This would make them appear less brutal and cynical than in the traditional

Western view, without at the same time blatantly distorting history as the Soviet interpretation tends to do. This approach would not be a variation on the theme of 'once a Bolshevik, always a Bolshevik' but rather on an acknowledgement that Bolshevik policies and objectives changed as the Party became a regime. Again, there are two possible approaches.

One is that a liberating power became corrupted by the terrible circumstances in which it found itself. This is especially the view of part of the political left in the West, or at least that part of it that has remained pro-Leninist. John Rees, for example, argues that the dissolution of the Constituent Assembly and the introduction of a one-party system can be explained by the enormous pressures confronting the Bolsheviks in 1918. How could they adhere to a policy of transforming the country if they allowed the Constituent Assembly to continue to exist as a 'rallying point for the right'? The terror can also be explained by reference to the pressures placed on the Bolsheviks. They were up against a wave of atrocities being committed by the Whites and the widespread threat of counter-revolution. Here the argument becomes particularly intriguing. 'The ultimate cause of the extent of Red Terror lies . . . in the isolation of the Russian working class. The sea of peasants were the element in which the counter-revolution swam. The SRs, who claimed to represent the peasantry, were the foremost promoters of counter-revolution behind Red lines.' Hence Lenin's use of terror, although out of line with his earlier policies, was a recognisable revolutionary process. Indeed, he was 'following the example of the French Revolution'.[11] He was also the first to recognise that the Cheka had outlived its usefulness once the Civil War had ceased to have a radicalising influence; this explains why he wound it up in 1922.

This case is certainly more prepared to accept Bolshevik responsibility for dark events within an unhappy and turbulent period than is the Soviet interpretation. Even so, it comes close in its own way to being polemical: at times it seeks to justify and defend as much as to explain and clarify. A more convincing argument that the Bolsheviks changed in the course of 1917 and 1918 has been put by Western revisionist historians who, one feels, are more interested in history than in sustaining positions in a civil war of historical interpretation between various factions of the political left. The essence of the Western revisionist view is that the Bolshevik approach to power *did* change – and that it changed voluntarily. During the course of 1917 the Bolshevik Party had been relatively democratic, and as such had been receptive to broader influences and to grass-roots opinion. From 1918, however, Lenin instituted a more rigid and authoritarian structure that aimed quite deliberately to remove other influences. The battleground was the Constituent Assembly, the Socialist Revolutionaries' control of which rivalled the Bolshevik hold on the Congress of Soviets. The confrontation that followed became an integral part of the Civil War and changed the direction of the October Revolution. Thus the period between 1918 and 1921 was neither the continuation of the liberating revolution of October (the Soviet view) nor the real revolution following the October coup (the traditional Western view). It was, if anything, intended to close down the October Revolution and to deny to non-Bolshevik revolutionaries any access to its changes or benefits. The Bolsheviks had therefore made a fundamental transition – from liberators to oppressors.

Economic changes

Interpretations of Bolshevik economic policies have to deal with the change of direction made by Lenin's regime from initial caution between October 1917 and the middle of 1918 to the more radical phase of War Communism (1918–21), and back to the moderation of the New Economic Policy, drawn up in 1921. There are three broad explanations for this apparent inconsistency.

The first is that Lenin's policy was instinctively fair and moderate but that it was affected – for a while – by the terrible situation caused by the Russian Civil War. The official Soviet view is that 'Soviet Russia entered the period of 'transition from capitalism to socialism' as had always been intended, but with a proper regard for caution. After all, Russia was the first country to attempt the change and 'there were no ready-made patterns for reorganising the economy along socialist lines'.[12] Unfortunately, more radical measures had to be taken during the Civil War to requisition grain to feed the population, although these were ended as quickly as possible. Lenin then focused attention on a period of recovery through the New Economic Policy. Admittedly, this was a sharp turn from War Communism but, in making it, the Party showed 'knowledge of the laws of social development' and 'the great Lenin showed his genius and scientific foresight'.[13] This version does make an uncharacteristic concession that Lenin did at times change his mind. (Indeed, he later admitted that 'War Communism was thrust upon us by war and ruin. It was not, nor could it be, a policy that corresponded to the economic tasks of the proletariat. It was a temporary measure.'[14]) This, of course, provides a credible reason for the switch to the NEP. In the process, however, it underestimates the extent of the opposition to War Communism from the entire peasantry and says little about the threats to the Bolshevik regime in 1921. To argue that War Communism was reversed because the war was over may appear logical, but it is misleading. War Communism damaged the war effort and did much to provoke the 'second Green phase' of the Civil War (see Chapter 6). A more convincing interpretation is therefore needed.

A second possibility is the opposite of the first: Lenin was instinctively radical and introduced an extreme policy that he later had to reverse. This view, put forward by Dmitri Volkogonov, is an example of a modern post-Soviet Russian perspective against the earlier official Soviet approach. 'War Communism has always been associated with the civil war, and considered as a temporary policy which could be abandoned and replaced by the New Economic Policy as easily as it had been adopted. In fact, it was the basis and essence of Lenin's policy, and only its total collapse forced him to grab the lifebelt of the NEP.'[15] Volkogonov also points out that War Communism remained an underlying alternative strategy that was revived in the Stalinist period and remained intact until Gorbachev's reforms of the 1980s. In this respect Lenin was directly responsible for the repressive system upon which the economy, like the government, came to be based.

A third line of argument, followed by most Western historians, is that Lenin had no economic strategy at all; rather the economic changes were connected with the political situation in which Lenin found himself at a particular time. There was therefore a strong element of pragmatism, just as there always had been before 1917, and his economic policies were again conditioned by considerations of power. Lenin may well have used the situation of the Civil War to impose economic discipline; hence, as Robert Conquest maintains, this was very much a minority policy, dictated from above. 'In fact, the Bolshevik policies had proved economically disastrous and their methods of enforcement politically detested by all classes'. This necessitated a swift change of course: the NEP was introduced only because the Bolsheviks were 'at the end of their tether'.[16] Lenin may also have convinced himself that the time was right to split the peasantry by distinguishing between the majority and the wealthy few, or kulaks. This was, after all, a strategy that he had already developed with some success to weaken support for the Socialist Revolutionaries.

Finally, it could be argued that the Bolshevik regime underwent a fundamental change of heart, moving from moderation to radicalism. The revisionist case is that the Bolsheviks had come to power in October broadly representing the wishes of most of the people. Their earliest measures, including the Decree on Land, were bound to reflect this. During the first half of 1918, however, the agreement between the Bolsheviks and other groups rapidly eroded during the 'first Green phase' of the Civil War (see Chapter 6). Hence the Bolsheviks changed from a broad-based approach to a narrow one. Their economic policy became more authoritarian as War Communism introduced requisitioning to force the peasantry to give up its grain while, at the same time, forcing upon the urban workforce a panoply of regulations, work books and labour camps. Edward Acton's summary is that 'During 1918, the autonomy and democratic processes of the popular organizations thrown up in the course of the revolution were steadily undermined.'[17] This can be shown by the spread of Party power to cover all of the economic decision-making processes. The failure of War Communism meant that the NEP had to be introduced as a temporary measure, but this concession was made possible by the Bolshevik monopoly of political power. Any economic concession was therefore cancelled out by the regime remaining a political dictatorship.

In this way the revisionist and more traditional western perspectives merge by 1921 so that it is from this point very difficult to tell them apart. But perhaps the revisionists have missed a trick or two. The following argument, couched in their terminology, could be added to explain the transition to and then away from War Communism.

The period between 1918 and 1921 continued to show a direct connection between 'top-down' and 'bottom-up' influences, although in a different way to the period leading up to October 1917. The Bolsheviks were more in control of the levers of power and less likely to adjust to the demands of the different sectors of the population; in this way, it is true, they had changed. But the relationship still existed and still continued to influence their policy. For example, War Communism may well have started from an awareness of grass-roots pressures. The local soviets were already taking over far more of the industrial concerns and enterprises than the government had authorised and there were already widespread complaints in factories about the high cost of living and shortage of necessities. Perhaps Lenin felt able to speed up the nationalisation of industry and to apply requisitioning against the peasantry in the belief that he had the support of the workers. Only this time he was articulating views from below through the full force of state power and not through party programmes. The problem was that the policy did not work. Again, the grass-roots pressure proved important. The wave of popular discontent in 1920 and 1921 – both rural and urban – sent the strongest signal to Lenin that voices from below were still able to make themselves heard. The NEP was an acknowledgement of this.

Conclusion

The potential for further debate is considerable. There has always been an underemphasis on the period 1918–24 by comparison with the more immediately significant event of October 1917. The problem of relating one to the other remains and, for once, revisionist arguments have not yet offered a complete alternative to other, more established views. Students, be aware.

Questions

1. Why do historians disagree about why the Bolsheviks introduced a one-party state between 1918 and 1924?
2. Which historical interpretation do you find most convincing for the Bolshevik economic changes between 1918 and 1924?

SOURCES

1. WHO IS THE ENEMY?

Source A: A Bolshevik poster of the Civil War period (1918–21).

[See following page]

Source B: Lenin's views on who will suppress whom in the future. This extract is from *State and Revolution*, written by Lenin in the summer of 1917.

During the transition from capitalism to Communism suppression is still necessary; but it is now the suppression of the exploiting minority by the exploited majority. A special apparatus, a special machine of suppression, the state, is still necessary, but it is now a transitory state. It is no longer a state in the proper sense, for the suppression of the minority of exploiters by the majority of the wage-slaves of yesterday is comparatively so easy, simple and natural a task that it will entail far less bloodshed. And it is compatible with the extension of democracy to such an overwhelming majority of the population that the need for a special machine of suppression will begin to disappear.

Source C: Official document establishing the strategy of the Cheka, 12 June 1918.

In view of the threatening and exceptional circumstances of the time the following resolutions are submitted:

Source A: A Bolshevik poster of the Civil War period (1918–21). Courtesy of the Novosti Photo Library.

1 To employ secret agents.
2 To withdraw from circulation the prominent and active leaders of the Monarchist-Kadets, Right SRs and Mensheviks.
3 To register and have shadowed the generals and officers, to put under surveillance the Red Army, the officer staff, clubs, circles, schools etc.
4 To execute prominent and clearly exposed counter-revolutionaries, speculators, robbers and bribe-takers.
5 In the provinces to adopt strict and decisive measures to suppress the distribution of the bourgeois, conciliationist and gutter press.

Source D: An account of an event in Moscow given by a British diplomat, Robert Bruce Lockhart.

I was reading in the afternoon, when Peters came into the room. He told me strange tales of his experiences as a revolutionary. He had been in prison in Riga in Tsarist days. He showed me his nails as proof of the torture which he had undergone.

As we were talking, a motor van – a kind of 'Black Maria' – pulled up in the courtyard below, and a squad of men, armed with rifles and bandoliers, got out and took up their places in the yard. Presently, a door opened just below us, and three men with bowed heads walked slowly forward to the van. They were Scheglovitoff, Khvostoff, and Belietsky, three ex-Ministers of the Tsarist regime, who had been in prison since the Revolution. There was a pause, followed by a scream. Then, through the door the fat figure of a priest was half-pushed, half-carried, to the 'Black Maria'. His terror was pitiful. Tears rolled down his face. His knees rocked, and he fell like a great ball of fat on the ground. I felt sick and turned away. 'Where are they going?' I asked. 'They are going to another world,' said Peters dryly. The ex-Ministers formed the first batch of the several hundred victims of the Terror who were shot at that time as a reprisal for the attempted assassination of Lenin.

Questions

1. Using these Sources and your own knowledge, explain the meaning and purpose of the Cheka. (20)
2. Compare the ideas shown in Sources A and B. To what extent are they being implemented in Source C? (40)
3. 'The Bolsheviks came to power promising liberty against oppression, only to become oppressors themselves.' Do these Sources and your own knowledge support this view? (60)

2. DID THE LENINIST STATE ABANDON DEMOCRACY?

Source E: A resolution of the Central Executive Committee dissolving the Constituent Assembly, 19 January 1918.

The Constituent Assembly, elected on the basis of lists drawn up before the October Revolution, was expressive of the old correlation of political forces, when the conciliators and Constitutional-Democrats were in power . . . Thus the Constituent Assembly, which was to have crowned the bourgeois parliamentary republic, was bound to stand in the way of the October Revolution and Soviet power.

The October Revolution, which gave power to the Soviets and through them to the working and exploited classes, aroused frantic resistance on the part of the exploiters . . . The working classes learned through experience that old bourgeois parliamentarism had outlived its day, that it was utterly incompatible with the tasks of Socialism, and that only class institutions (such as the Soviets) and not national ones were capable of overcoming the resistance of the propertied classes and laying the foundations of socialist society.

Any renunciation of the sovereign power of the Soviets, of the Soviet Republic won by the people, in favour of bourgeois parliamentarism and the Constituent Assembly would now be a step backwards and would cause a collapse of the entire October Workers' and Peasants' Revolution . . .

In view of this, the Central Executive Committee resolves:

The Constituent Assembly is hereby dissolved.

Source F: Extract from *A Short History of the Communist Party of the Soviet Union*, published under the direction of the Soviet government (1970 edition).

The position and role of the Communist Party changed with the triumph of the October Revolution. From a Party devoted to the overthrow and destruction of the old system it became a Party dedicated to building a new society without exploiters, without oppression of man by man . . .

The Bolshevik Party became the ruling Party of the world's first socialist state, but it did not refuse to co-operate with other political parties, provided they accepted the decisions of the Second Congress of Soviets and the platform of the Soviet government set up by that supreme organ of people's representatives . . . The Socialist Revolutionaries and the Mensheviks rejected the Bolshevik proposal.

After the working class had seized power, Lenin said, the Party's main task was to learn to administer the country. This was an art that the workers and peasants could not simply adopt from the bourgeoisie. The state apparatus created by it could not be utilised. The bourgeois state and its apparatus had been set up and improved with the purpose of keeping the working people in subjugation. It had to be completely abolished and a state created without and against the bourgeoisie, i.e., a state of the dictatorship of the proletariat founded on co-operation between the workers and peasants . . .

Defeated in open battle, the counter-revolutionary Constitutional-Democratic, Right Socialist-Revolutionary and Menshevik parties planned to overthrow Soviet rule through the Constituent Assembly . . . The people expected the Constituent Assembly to confirm the gains of the October Revolution and the decrees and decisions of the Second Congress of Soviets. At the Constituent Assembly, which opened early in January 1918, the Bolsheviks and Left Socialist-Revolutionaries tabled a motion calling for recognition of the fact that all power in the land was vested in the Soviets and for the endorsement of the decrees on peace and on land and the peace-loving foreign policy of the Soviet Government. This meant recognising what the people had already approved. But the Right Socialist-Revolutionary majority in the Assembly refused even to debate this motion, thereby setting itself above the will of the people. Soviet power was compelled to disband the Assembly.

Source G: Extract from Rex Wade, *The Russian Revolution, 1917*, published 2000. At the time of writing, the author was Professor of History at George Mason University, Virginia.

Dispersing the Constituent Assembly was one of the most fateful decisions Lenin was ever to make. The results for the Bolsheviks, Russia and the world were of a significance almost impossible to exaggerate. For the Bolsheviks, in the immediate situation, it appeared merely that they had avoided a serious threat to their hold on power. More fundamentally, however, it revealed that the party had irrevocably set itself upon the course of dictatorial rule and that those members who had protested that tendency in November had given up their 'constitutional illusions', as Lenin derisively called them. The party would cling to power at any price and take the road of authoritarian government and dictatorship.

The consequences for Russia were even more profound. By this act Lenin and his party announced clearly that they were abandoning the long-held intelligentsia commitment to the people's right to express through the ballot their wishes on fundamental political issues. More specifically, the dispersal of the Constituent Assembly was an announcement by the Bolsheviks that they would not give up governmental authority peacefully, via elections, but could be removed only by force. To the misfortune of millions of people, this meant that civil war was inevitable . . .

Nor was that an end to it, for the long-run repercussions were equally great . . . January 6 . . . witnessed not merely the end of the Russian Revolution, but the destruction of the democratic and constitutional hopes that had fitfully resided there since 1906 and which appeared to have finally been realized in the heady days of spring 1917. The Bolsheviks' decision to abandon the electoral politics of 1917 and rule by force laid the foundations of the political culture of the Soviet Union.

Source H: Extract from John Rees, 'In Defence of October', an essay published in *International Socialism* in 1997. At the time of publication the author was editor of *International Socialism* and a leading member of the Socialist Workers Party in Britain.

The dissolution of the Constituent Assembly by the Bolsheviks in January 1918 is one of their most contentious acts. The essential problem [with criticisms of this act] is that they ask the question: if we were the founding fathers of the workers' constitution, what democratic blueprint would we propose? The question they do *not* ask is: in the struggle for power which institutions represent the interests of the workers and which the interests of the ruling class? These questions need careful analysis in the revolutionary period because the role of the different institutions alters dramatically depending on the balance of class forces . . .

Even before the October revolution the mass of workers understood clearly that the soviets were their organisations, responsive to their needs, and that the Assembly was a chimera of which they knew very little and from which they expected less . . .

A parliament could be a rallying point for the bourgeoisie during their revolution precisely because they aimed only at *political* power. In general they were already masters, or near masters of the economy. The bourgeoisie and the SRs clearly understood this and were keen to restore all the old separations inherent in a bourgeois state as the first step on the road to counter-revolution. The Constituent Assembly was a rallying point for the right.

Questions

1. Analyse and explain the similarities between the explanations within Sources E and F for the dissolution of the Constituent Assembly in January 1918. (15)
*2. Using Sources E to H, explain why historians have disagreed over whether Lenin and the Bolsheviks introduced dictatorship to or preserved democracy in Russia from 1918. (30)

Worked answer

*2. In theory, at least, dictatorship and democracy are far apart in the political spectrum. There are, however, major differences in definition for both terms, as is shown by Sources E to H, which range from an original explanation for abolishing the Constituent Assembly, through a later Soviet justification for this action, to two more recent comments.

The original justification given by the Bolsheviks for the regime introduced in 1918 was that it was more genuinely democratic than the one it replaced. This is the point of Source E, with its focus on the substitution of 'Soviet power' for a 'bourgeois parliamentary republic'. The latter, represented by the Constituent Assembly was antidemocratic in being 'the old correlation of political forces'. This may appear a logical argument for the ideological approach of Marxism–Leninism, with its emphasis on the movement towards Communism via the 'dictatorship of the proletariat'. But it is also somewhat disingenuous, as a key factor in the adoption of the Soviet system was practical: the defeat of the Bolsheviks in the elections to the Constituent Assembly. It is hardly surprising that the 'official Soviet' interpretation should have perpetuated the myth that Lenin had introduced a 'higher' form of democracy, since this underlay the whole political structure of soviet system of the USSR – at least until the political reforms of Gorbachev in the late 1980s. Hence Source F was bound to reinforce Source E by focusing on 'building a new society without exploiters' in which there would be 'co-operation between workers and peasants'; the old order, based on the Constituent Assembly and the 'counter-revolutionary parties' simply had to go. The future Soviet regime depended for its legitimacy on developments like this, and the Short History of the CPSU built up a retrospective justification in terms of 'democratic centralism' and 'dictatorship of the proletariat'.

Most Western historians have applied the reverse interpretation: the abolition of the Constituent Assembly was a decisive step away from democracy and towards dictatorship. This was because the Bolsheviks ended any plural approach to politics, substituting instead a one-party state. Source G, for example, maintains that the 'party had irrevocably set itself upon the course of dictatorial rule', with 'profound' consequences for Russia's future. The move was also antidemocratic since it abandoned elections 'through the ballot' and created a regime that 'could be removed only by force'. In contrast with their discussions on many other issues, Western historians, whether 'liberal' or 'revisionist', show an unusual consensus about the new regime being a dictatorship. This is due largely to the way in which democracy has come to be defined in the West. It is seen as an open society that allows diversity (including historical debate based on academic criteria) and resists single-issue political solutions. Systems that remove choice are, by contrast, seen as 'dictatorships'. If there is a debate on what the Bolsheviks did in 1918, it rests more on whether they were *always* inclined to dictatorship (as 'Western liberal' historians believe) or whether they suddenly switched to dictatorship in 1918 (as 'Western revisionists' tend to argue). The liberal historians, more influenced by the atmosphere of the Cold War, tend to see the Bolsheviks as long-term conspirators whipped into shape by the evil genius of Lenin, while the revisionists see Lenin brought to power on a wave of democratic support in October 1917, but closing down the democratic process in 1918. There is, in other words, an academic debate as to whether dictatorship was inherent to Bolshevism.

Yet not all non-Soviet opinion would be so tempted to dismiss Lenin's regime as a dictatorship. Some 'Western Marxist' historians have defended Lenin's system of soviets on the grounds of necessity and practicality – as an imperfect way of preserving elements of democracy while doing away with some of the democratic processes. Sympathies have been expressed by such biographers of Lenin as Christopher Hill, or by more openly political historians, such as the author of Source H. The latter adopts an unqualified defence of Lenin's actions, casting the argument in terms of everything depends on 'the balance of class forces'; the suppression of the Constituent Assembly can be justified because it was 'a rallying point for the right'. Reasons for Western Marxist viewpoints might range from the academic use of infrastructural analysis, based on class conflict, to a more polemical projection of the aims of a modern political party.

Terms such as 'dictatorship' and 'democracy' have always been difficult to define. When attached to historical figures such as Lenin they provoke the type of controversy that give history the additional layer of historiography.

8

WHICH LENIN?

BACKGROUND

Chapters 3 to 7 have covered the development of Bolshevik power, under Lenin's leadership, through the key stages between 1898 and 1924. The period to 1903 saw the emergence of the Social Democrats and the split between Bolsheviks and Mensheviks (Chapter 3). Between 1903 and February 1917 Lenin tried to find a meaningful role for a more radicalised Bolshevik Party (Chapter 4), eventually coming to power in October 1917 (Chapter 5), dealing with attempts to overthrow Bolshevik rule (Chapter 6) and altering the nature of the revolution between 1918 and 1924 (Chapter 7). Each phase has been considered in terms of its history and historiography. A preliminary overall perspective was provided in Chapter 2, while Chapter 1 provided reasons for some of the differences of opinion that go to make up historiography.

It is now necessary to pull together the threads of interpretation concerning Lenin himself. Two issues are of particular importance here. How much influence did he exert on events at the time? And how important was his subsequent legacy? In both cases the varying opinions and interpretations will invite the more general question: 'Which is the *real* Lenin?'

ANALYSIS (1): DISCUSS THE VARIOUS VIEWS ON LENIN'S CONTRIBUTIONS TO THE ESTABLISHMENT OF COMMUNISM IN RUSSIA.

Interpretations will vary according to the degree of importance given to the role of the individual in history. This, in turn, will depend on the purpose, scope and context of the writing involved. Any analysis will involve some consideration of the influence of the individual and of other factors – but the balance between the two is the critical factor. By and large, the emphasis will tend to polarise towards either the individual being predominantly the *direct* agent of change or the individual being the *indirect* agent.

For many historians it would be impossible to envisage the development of Marxism within Russia or the establishment of a Communist regime without the direct involvement of Lenin. His involvement was overriding in terms of intellectual influence, leadership and intention.

The importance of Lenin's writings

First, Lenin was probably the most prolific writer that Marxism has ever had. His collected works amount to over twenty volumes and seem to cover all the different aspects of revolutionary activity. But how important were Lenin's ideas in creating a revolution? It is certainly possible to see his works as a sequence of stages in the development of the Social Democratic movement and the Bolshevik Party. His *Tasks of the Russian Social Democrats* (1898) suggested a programme for a united Marxist party, while *The Development of Capitalism in Russia* (1899) showed how Marxism might be adapted to Russian conditions. *What Is to Be Done?* (1902) provided a structure for a revolutionary party with limited membership, clear objectives and professional leadership. His *One Step Forward, Two Steps Back* (1904) attacked the alternative Menshevik strategy of collaborating with other opponents of the Tsarist regime, a theme that was further developed in *Two Tactics of Social Democracy in the Democratic Revolution* (1905). Meanwhile, *To the Rural Poor* (1903) had established a link between the proletariat and the lower stratum of the peasantry as the main revolutionary classes. *Imperialism: The Highest Stage of Capitalism* (1915) seemed to provide a conscious decision regarding how a conflict between capitalist regimes could be used to accelerate people's revolution. Once the Tsarist regime had been brought down Lenin was able to articulate popular demands more directly in his *April Theses* (April 1917), while also emphasising the need for a disciplined approach to introducing the Marxist phase of the 'dictatorship of the proletariat': this was apparent in *The State and Revolution* (1917).

Of course, the importance of these writings can be seen in different ways. One possibility is that they acted as a blueprint (or redprint?) for the development of Communism in Russia. The official Soviet view is that Lenin was at the same time part of a general historical trend but sole interpreter of that trend. His importance was that, in recognising what was historically inevitable, he made the inevitable happen: in this way he made history. The official biography of Lenin is full of references to his intellect and deeper understanding. For example, his interpretation of the economy in *The Development of Capitalism in Russia* 'dealt the deathblow' to Russia's other revolutionary tradition,[1] populism, and set in motion the trend towards Marxism. *What Is to Be Done?* and *Two Tactics of Social Democracy in the Democratic Revolution* show Lenin at his creative best, designing 'an entirely different kind of party, a truly revolutionary party capable of organising and leading the working class of Russia to the assault of the Tsarist autocracy and capitalism'.[2] His strategy of using the First World War to hasten the revolution (as argued in *Imperialism: The Highest Stage of Capitalism*) was 'a great scientific discovery of tremendous significance',[3] while *The State and Revolution* gave all the necessary guidance for the future, providing a 'clear understanding of what the workers' and peasants' state should be like and what programme the Soviet government should carry out.'[4] Overall, Lenin's intellect clarified the situation Russia that was in and showed the way in which it could be changed.

A second alternative is that Lenin was using ideas to justify, rather than plan, his policy. His ideas were reactive rather than proactive and were based on pragmatic considerations such as the justification of autocratic leadership. The majority of Western historians have seen Lenin as a manipulator rather than a creator. His earlier works, especially *What Is to Be Done?* and *Two Tactics* were motivated by a struggle for power within the Marxist movement and by a reversion to the conspiratorial approach endemic to Russian revolutionary traditions. *Imperialism: The Highest Stage of Capitalism* was little more than the opportunist use of the First World War to destabilise a regime that was otherwise impossible to shift. The *April Theses* were similarly a pragmatic shift of policy, partly at the expense of earlier ideology, to encourage the people to desert their allegiance to the Socialist Revolutionaries and Mensheviks. Once this happened, Lenin made it clear in *The State and Revolution* that he preferred dictatorship as a style of government for the future. All of this was powerful and effective not as creative or scientific ideology but rather as a means of keeping control and power.

A third possibility – pointed out by the revisionist trend, both in Russia and the West – is to see other influences at work on Lenin's ideas, which he eventually articulated in his writings. Unlike earlier Western historians, they argue that many of the ideas were probably genuine and probably did represent the aspirations of substantial sectors of the population. Unlike the official Soviet view, however, the revisionists see the origins of these ideas less in Lenin's intellect than in the influences welling up from the grass roots. This happened at various stages. His early views on Marxism were already being anticipated by educated members of activist committees of workers in factories. His insistence on conspiratorial methods and tight leadership reflected methods already practised in the wave of strikes in 1903. His strategy for 'turning the imperialist war into a civil war' had previously been discussed in numerous non-Bolshevik works, while the *April Theses* were based substantially on petitions worked out by committees representing the peasantry, factory workers and soldiers once they had begun to suspect that the Provisional Government was not delivering what they actually wanted.

Which of these interpretations is the most likely? The Soviet and mainstream Western views have in common a profound deference to Lenin's writings, although obviously for different reasons. In retrospect they may well appear to take Lenin's views too seriously. To accept the Soviet approach requires a belief in the ideology and mythology which go with it, and a willingness to elevate polemical writing to biblical proportions. Since the collapse in 1991 of the regime that the dogma inspired few serious analysts are still prepared to do this. By contrast, the 'evil-genius' approach, always preferred in the West, still has widespread backing. Again, however, it reads too much into ideas that are often blurred and contradictory. Revisionist historians have succeeded in cutting Lenin down to size as an original intellectual with the capacity to inspire or dominate; it is certainly intriguing – and not a little paradoxical – to see the great leader following the common people. But have they gone too far? Post-revisionist views are already reasserting the direct importance of his intellectual influence.

The importance of Lenin as an organiser and leader

History is littered with revolutions which have failed. The Bolshevik Revolution has now become one of these, but only in the longer-term perspective. Within the context of the twentieth century it was of crucial importance and, for much of that period, it was unthinkable to question the direct agency of Lenin's organisation and leadership. For Soviet and non-Soviet historians alike, the way in which he carried out the revolution was as important as the ideas driving him forward.

The Soviet view showed, as always, total adulation. His organisation covered every area: indeed, Marxism–Leninism could be seen as Marxism with a practical structure, as 'a mighty vehicle for the revolutionary transformation of the world'.[5] Lenin therefore provided the 'science of revolutionary leadership'. He stressed the importance of obedience, discipline and total commitment to the Party, since only in this way could the Bolsheviks be 'the vanguard' of revolutionary action. 'Democratic centralism' was the key factor, combining organisation with representation of the masses. After all, 'scattered actions by individual groups have never brought victory'.[6] One of Lenin's greatest organisational achievements was to establish the link between the urban workers (the vanguard of the revolution) and the peasantry (the reserve). Lenin developed activism where it was most needed, in the form of strike action to paralyse industry, and mutinies to undermine the Tsarist war effort. He was also at the forefront in developing the means of spreading ideas and information, first through *Iskra*, later through *Pravda*. Organisation was also used to identify the enemy, which Lenin did with clarity and precision. The Mensheviks were 'opportunists and dogmatists, who turned a blind eye to reality and feared victory';[7] the parties of the bourgeoisie tried to 'steal' the victory of others, while the Socialist Revolutionaries were of the 'petty bourgeoisie', obsessed with private property. Lenin's greatest leadership qualities were shown in times of apparent adversity. Hence he drove the Party to recovery after the setback of the 1905 Revolution and insisted on the seizure of power in October 1917, only weeks after the Bolshevik headquarters had been raided by the Provisional Government. According to the official Soviet biography of Lenin, the October Revolution showed 'Lenin's genius as a leader of the masses' as well as a 'wise and fearless strategist who clearly saw what direction the revolution would take'.[8] Lenin was also directly responsible for saving Bolshevik Russia from the 'whiteguards' and their allies, as well as for implementing the principle of 'democratic centralism' in a new type of state based on soviets rather than 'bourgeois institutions'.

Much of this is instantly recognisable as propaganda produced by a later regime seeking to secure its own credibility. It is therefore difficult to establish whether Lenin's achievements were recognised by future regimes acting upon them or read back by those regimes to the man they saw as their architect. Whatever the case, this image of Lenin as a powerful individual leader has also had an impact on the West, although non-Soviet historians have been much more critical of the way in which Lenin deployed his abilities. Again, there is no questioning his influence in forming a revolutionary party, although Western historians tend to see this as conspiratorial and based very much on the notion of a minority incorrectly claiming to be acting on behalf of the majority. Lenin created not so much a vanguard as a clique. According to Merle Fainsod, 'The Bolshevik Revolution was not a majoritarian movement.' But it did not need to be. 'The enemies of Bolshevism were numerous, but they were also weak, poorly organized, divided and apathetic.' What really counted were the strategy and leadership of Lenin. 'The strategy of Lenin was calculated to emphasize their divisions, neutralize their opposition, and capitalize on their apathy. In 1902 in *What Is to Be Done?* Lenin had written, "Give us an organization of revolutionaries, and we shall overturn the whole of Russia!" On November 7, 1917, the wish was fulfilled and the deed accomplished.'[9] Other historians take further the emphasis on what could be done by a disciplined minority under ruthless leadership. The Bolshevik regime, J.L.H. Keep maintained, pretended to be democratic, but 'Common to all soviets was a form of organization that permitted them to be influenced – indeed, manipulated – by the radical activists.'[10] Through all of this, Lenin showed that he was really a Jacobin. In the words of Richard Pipes, 'his strategy owed precious little to Marxism and everything to an insatiable lust for power'.[11] That he got away with it is, according to Adam Ulam, a reflection on the lack of political awareness among the population at large.[12]

Three assumptions arise from this somewhat more critical approach to Lenin. One is that Lenin was a cynical manipulator of power and that ideology was little more than a front for his own supremacy, first within the Party and then within the state. However, this is a better description of Stalin, which again raises the question of whether history is being read backwards. A second is that the Bolsheviks were in Lenin's grip and driven by his demonic zeal. Yet it is very rare for leadership that effective to emerge, especially in a country with a long tradition of failed conspiracies. Third, the Russian people at the beginning of the century are not given much credit in terms of political awareness and development. This contrasts with the general acknowledgement given to the growing importance of the influence of the masses in Britain, Germany, France and Italy.

These points are addressed by revisionist historians both in Russia and in the West. Their main achievement has been to redress a perceived imbalance between an all-powerful individual leader and a largely inert and exploited population. As we have seen, the emphasis of revisionists is to restore to the people at least some of the initiative for historical trends, so that the influence for change has a 'bottom-up' as well as a 'top-down' perspective. All parts of the population had elements that were politically aware. As T. Shanin has shown,[13] this applied especially to the peasantry, previously thought to have been almost impervious to political radicalism. The army, too, was well shaken by its rank and file – irrespective of what Lenin was urging them to do.[14] We have already seen that small revolutionary groups and strike committees in factories fed ideas upwards for Lenin to articulate in more detail in some of his writings. This means that Lenin's leadership must have had widespread support, although not for the reasons given by the Soviet historians. At the same time, the Bolshevik Party cannot have been as tightly structured as the more traditional Western views suggest. Lenin was simply unable to prevent divisions from appearing (as can be seen with the heated debate in October about the seizure of power). If anything, the Bolsheviks were best placed to take power at the time that the Party was most influenced by the grass roots and acting with radical groups from other parties. Thus, Lenin did not lead the masses into action with a vanguard force showing them their direction and targets. Nor did he seize power with a clique while most of the population were asleep. According to the revisionist view, he went with the popular flow and, by following the trend, appeared to lead it.

Revisionism is by definition new and often radical. It also takes time to settle down – by which time it has often become orthodox. Elements of the revisionist approach are clearly here to stay. They have shown that individuals are open to more influences than had previously been thought and that the clearest view of an individual's role in a particular situation can be obtained by looking at it from the periphery rather than from the centre. This is probably why most revisionists have produced monographs and specialist studies rather than mainstream biographies. Revisionism has also shown that 'efficiency' and 'organisation' are deceptive concepts, especially when applied to parties and regimes, and that no leader can expect unqualified success in applying them. Yet the initial attack of revisionism on entrenched positions probably went too far, threatening, in its enthusiasm, to throw Lenin out with the backwater. This is why it has already attracted strong criticism from earlier historians such as Richard Pipes for blurring the main focus while concentrating on the periphery.

The importance of objective influences

We have seen that Lenin's importance has been elevated from time to time by the type of writing that has focused on him. Soviet propaganda, for example, required a hero, while traditional Western biographies required a personal focus; whether this revealed a hero or a villain depended on the perspective of the author. There is, however, a very different approach to Lenin's involvement in the historical process between 1898 and 1924. This stresses the importance of other influences over which Lenin had far less control. Some of these have always been acknowledged, as much by the biographers emphasising Lenin's individuality as by anyone else.

There are several obvious examples of Lenin taking advantage of events working in his favour; these can be found in any work produced in the west on Lenin, whether traditional or revisionist. One is the weakening of the Tsarist regime – and then of the Provisional Government – by the destabilising influence of the First World War. In both cases, but especially the latter, Lenin benefited enormously, finding the means to give the Bolsheviks a new sense of purpose and direction. Another example is the deepening crisis faced by the Provisional Government. Lenin was able to exploit the growing disillusionment of substantial parts of the population with the inability of the various coalitions to deliver promised reforms. He also benefited from the splits appearing within such middle-class parties as the Cadets and Octobrists, as well as in rivals from the left – the Mensheviks and Socialist Revolutionaries. Similarly, the lack of a combined opposition to the Bolshevik regime enabled him to seize victory and dictatorship from the chaos of the Civil War. The official Soviet view is that all of these were symptomatic of a broad historical trend. They were not so much objective factors working in Lenin's failure as conditions created by his assault on a weakening assailant. Western historians – whether traditional or revisionist – would give far more emphasis to the operation of chance, coincidence and complex interaction.

Revisionism, however, has added to the range of objective influences, in the process further reducing the extent to which Lenin can be considered to have exerted direct control over events. One of these, already looked at in other contexts, is the influence of grass-roots radicalism. Consider the two crucial periods when Lenin consciously shifted the direction the party was to take; in each case he was definitely encouraged, and may well have been motivated by, popular action. In 1903 his stand on revolutionary activism was at least partly influenced by the general strike taking place in southern Russia at the same time as the London Congress, while the *April Theses* of 1917, so crucial to increasing the Party's popularity, were a direct response to popular demands expressed through local committees and petitions.

Another key objective influence on Lenin's seizure of power concerns the role of other parties in the events leading up to October 1917. In part, this is a traditional argument. It has always been acknowledged that the Socialist Revolutionaries and Mensheviks alienated large sections of the population because of their continuing association with an ailing Provisional Government. But there is now a revisionist corollary to this. Historians such as Rex Wade have shown that it is incorrect to claim that Lenin presided over a tightly disciplined and organised party that was unlike any other.[15] The real source of its strength in 1917 was actually the weakening of its centralised power, against all the efforts made by Lenin to hold it together. As a result, the Bolshevik Party became more democratic and open to ideas, which increased its standing in the Petrograd Soviet. Particularly important was the radical coalition that emerged from the fracturing of normal party loyalties. The Mensheviks and Socialist Revolutionaries both developed offshoots, which linked up with the Bolsheviks. Although the Bolsheviks themselves managed to avoid a direct split, there was strong internal disagreement on the timing of the revolution and on the type of regime to follow. All this offers a dramatic contrast to the traditional picture of Lenin as the leader of a disciplined Bolshevik strike-force against the well-intentioned but dithering moderate socialists. Instead, Lenin presided over a broad coalition of radicals, comprising the Bolsheviks, Menshevik-Internationalists and Left SRs, which competed for power against the moderate socialists, or Revolutionary Defencists. In this way Lenin is seen as becoming part of a broad trend that occurred between March and October 1917, which involved the radicalisation of the people and the realignment of radical parties to meet them.

A third example of a relatively 'new' objective factor assisting Lenin took place in 1918 during the Civil War. This is emphasised by the revisionist historians, but is scarcely mentioned by the traditional Western historians or in the official Soviet view. During the course of 1918, argues Geoffrey Swain,[16] the main threat to the continuation of Bolshevik power was the establishment of rival Green governments by the Socialist Revolutionaries. They attracted more widespread support and seemed to be stretching the Bolsheviks to the limit. What saved Lenin and the Reds was the emergence of the White counter-revolution – because these Green governments were overthrown in a series of White military coups, the most important being the collapse of the Ufa regime to Kolchak. Lenin found it much easier to deal with the attacks by the Whites because the latter lacked the popularity and legitimacy of the Greens; they were therefore enemies rather than rivals. The intriguing conclusion seems to be that different groups have different levels of power and pose different threats in accordance with which other groups they are threatening. Hence the Greens were a threat to the Reds, but not to the Whites, while the Whites were a threat to the Greens, but not, ultimately, to the Reds. Lenin could not possibly have asked for a better combination. In this respect he was indeed fortunate.

Conclusion

Historians have not yet finished with Lenin and the debate will continue as to whether his personal intervention and leadership were more important than objective factors in the rise of Soviet Communism. However, it is possible that arguments about this will follow a dialectical pattern and tend eventually towards a broad synthesis – only to be challenged by new variants. There has never been a better time for the student and general reader to take part in this process, and possibly to anticipate future conclusions.

Questions

1. Why do historians differ in their assessments of whether Lenin was 'in control' of the Bolshevik Revolution and the Bolshevik regime?
2. Which assessment of Lenin's role between 1903 and 1924 do you find most convincing?

ANALYSIS (2): HOW AND WHY HAVE HISTORIANS DIFFERED IN THEIR INTERPRETATION OF LENIN'S LEGACY TO RUSSIAN HISTORY?

The historiographical focus on Lenin's legacy after 1924 has been both simple and complex. The issues themselves are relatively straightforward and can be contained within two questions. Did Lenin exert any real influence on the leaders and regimes that followed him? And was any such influence positive and benign – or negative and malign? However, the answers to these questions have been complex, because virtually every historical school has gone through different combinations of answers. In this Analysis, they are best examined individually.

The official Soviet view and its collapse

The official Soviet view until the mid-1980s was that Lenin's influence was paramount for all phases of Soviet development after 1924. 'In all its day-to-day activities the CPSU is invariably guided by the life-evoking ideas of Lenin, which it creatively develops and applies in practice.'[17] This, however, contained a problem. None of Lenin's successors had this enduring sort of reputation. Each leader of the Soviet Union claimed a direct link with Lenin's ideas while, at the same time, denouncing his predecessor for breaking that connection. Hence Stalin (1929–53) attacked the records of Zinoviev and Kamenev; Khrushchev (1953–64) demolished Stalin's reputation, only to be demoted in turn by Brezhnev (1964–82). Yet whatever personal animosity they felt towards their predecessors, neither Khrushchev nor Brezhnev could argue that no progress had taken place under their leadership – since the absence of progress would have been a denial of Lenin's legacy. This posed a dilemma, the solution of which was the ruthless manipulation of history for political purposes. Once Stalin had been denounced by Khrushchev as a 'psychotic' dictator who distorted Lenin's aims, he was erased from the entire period 1929–53, and all credit for progress and development during this time was given to 'the Party'. This, of course, involved a monstrous distortion. 'The Party' had, under Stalin, been greatly weakened by his personalised dictatorship and was never in any position to undertake the collective leadership now ascribed to it. But the new formula gave the Soviet system a more positive past and re-established the connection with Lenin.

For the Soviet leadership, Lenin's influence therefore existed at two levels. The first was immediate: each of the Soviet leaders sought to base his political legitimacy on a direct link with Lenin. The second was retrospective. This involved a rewriting of history to eradicate the part played by past leaders who had 'distorted' Lenin and to salvage the idea that progress had occurred under Lenin's continuing inspiration. Thus the *Short History of the Communist Party of the Soviet Union* covered the Stalin period under such chapter headings as 'Lenin's Plan of Socialist Construction is Realised'. Although the details were readily provided by Khrushchev in 1956 and 1960, the *History* contained no references to mass starvation or to the widespread terror. These had been Stalin's fault – and Stalin's existence was no longer recognised.

The 1980s brought two key changes within the Soviet Union to the way in which Lenin was perceived. Both of these were the result of the *glasnost* introduced as a deliberate policy by Gorbachev (1985–91) to allow for more open debate. The first was to free Soviet history from political control and restore to Russia its real past. Stalin was featured in gory detail and new material was released on the extent of the purges and gulag system during his era. The second change was a consequence of the first. The dictatorship of Stalin was seen increasingly as an extreme form of the Leninist structure rather than as a departure from it. Soviet revisionist historians therefore began to question whether the role of Lenin had been quite so inspirational as previously thought. More credit was given to spontaneous popular involvement in the 1917 revolutions and links were beginning to be made between Lenin and Stalin. Following the collapse of the Soviet Union in 1991 Russian historians went further and began to project Lenin as a negative figure. Dmitri Volkogonov, for example, produced in 1994 a biography of Lenin which was searingly critical.[18] It established a direct connection between Lenin and all the repressive components of the Stalinist regime, concluding that the erosion of Leninism was accelerated by the reforms of Gorbachev and that the 'epoch of Lenin is gone for ever'.

Interpretations from the non-Soviet left

The official Soviet view was, by definition, produced by the establishment which grew up over several phases after the death of Lenin. This was initially dominated by Stalin. There were, however, other left-wing interpretations of Lenin's legacy, ranging from the historical writings of Trotsky through to the observations of Western Marxists.

Leon Trotsky had considerable influence on the left in the West. By pointing out the deficiencies of the Stalinist regime, he made it clear that Lenin's revolutionary momentum was not being followed in the Soviet Union, which instead had settled into the rut of bureaucratic and personal dictatorship. Trotsky continued to press for revolution outside Russia, although he was obliged to change Lenin's strategy of pressure through a single revolutionary party to a more pragmatic one of 'entryism', or operating covertly within other parties. It could be argued that this allowed Lenin at least some influence within the European left. Or Trotsky's approach could be seen as proof that Leninism could not survive outside the new mainstream of Stalinism.

British left-wing historians were initially united in their view that Lenin was a benign influence on Russia and the world but divided over whether Stalin provided continuity with the system Lenin had created. Some saw Stalin as a necessary evil for the material completion of Lenin's work, while others considered that he was a distortion of everything that Lenin had stood for. During the 1980s and 1990s, however, the consensus was that Stalinism was essentially negative and the debate switched to whether Lenin had already destroyed progressive influences before 1924. According to Samuel Farber, he had: by 1921, and certainly by 1923, 'soviet democracy no longer existed'.[19] This applied to Russia's political institutions, the press, workers' institutions and trade unions.

Modern European Communist leaders – some of whom are historians – tend to see a close connection between Lenin and Stalin; they also reject both Lenin and Stalin as irrelevant to their objectives. Manuel Azcarate, spokesman for the Spanish Communist Party, maintained that after the death of Lenin the word 'Leninism' was used as 'an instrument of legitimation' by the 'various factions which have sought to gain or retain control of the Communism Party of the Soviet Union'.[20] Ellenstein, a historian and one of the leaders of the French Communist Party in the 1980s, was more direct in his criticism. 'The Stalin phenomenon', he argued, 'arose from the Bolshevik revolution'; although relevant to Russia's earlier needs, 'Leninism and Stalinism can offer no guidelines to us.'[21] The reason for this line is the search for full acceptance and integration of Communist parties within Western-style democracy. It was felt during the 1970s and 1980s that Stalinist parties which owed their allegiance to Moscow were doomed to extinction. All influences behind the creation of the Soviet monolith had therefore to be bypassed if the Communist parties of Spain, Italy and France were to be more widely accepted. This meant recognising Lenin as the forebear of the Stalinist system and bypassing both in the return to a reinterpreted form of Marx.

Interpretations of Western non-Marxist historians

Non-Marxist historians of the West have also produced a variety of interpretations of Lenin's legacy, again based on variations of the theme that it was direct or indirect, positive or negative.

The earliest observers, in the 1920s, usually had personal reasons for their views of Lenin's regime and its influence and were either strongly in favour of Lenin or strongly against him. Max Eastman was a typical example of a writer with some sympathy towards Lenin.[22] He knew Lenin personally and stayed in Russia between 1922 and 1924. He was also the first Western observer to attack Stalin's regime and to take the side of Trotsky as a more natural successor to Lenin. In particular, he leaked the contents of Lenin's Political Testament, which had been given orally to him by Trotsky; this meant that from early on a number of Western historians used Soviet documentation and their acquaintance with some of the protagonists to argue that Stalin was an aberration of Lenin. Very much the same applied to those who saw a direct connection between Lenin and Stalin. Alexander Kerensky, for example, maintained that the Provisional Government had been overthrown by a criminal conspiracy that had then established itself under a repressive regime in a direct line from Lenin to Stalin. Kerensky, of course, had the strongest of reasons for his negative view of Lenin's legacy: trying to salvage his own reputation.

The 1930s, again, produced a split verdict. Some historians followed the same line as the playwright George Bernard Shaw in seeing the Soviet Union as a hive of purposeful construction and progress, with Stalin's planning system achieving the more nebulous ideals of Lenin. Others took more note of the sinister developments in the Soviet Union and saw in the purges and activities of the NKVD a confirmation that Lenin's Cheka had been reactivated and expanded. Unfortunately, neither approach was based on much evidence that was independently verifiable: instead, they depended substantially on Soviet propaganda and selective information or on hearsay and anti-Soviet sources.

The period between the end of the Second World War and the 1960s brought an unprecedented wave of writing in the West on both Lenin and Stalin. This was due to growing tensions between the West and the Soviet Union. The Cold War produced a range of works broadly hostile to Stalin that also traced the roots of Stalinist dictatorship to the Bolshevik regime of Lenin. Some distinguished between the 'authoritarianism' of Lenin and the 'totalitarianism' of Stalin, but saw, nevertheless, a direct connection between the two. This applies particularly to the work of Merle Fainsod.[23]

When Khrushchev released specific documentation denouncing Stalin in 1956, and again in 1960, there was a further change. Revelations of the true extent of Stalin's dictatorship, along with the thawing of the Cold War after 1962, tended to produce more diversity in Western interpretation. The focus on the evils of Stalinism was so intense that Lenin sometimes paled into insignificance by comparison. Robert Conquest, for example, was far more interested in Stalin's organisation of the 'Great Terror' than in any longer-term influences Lenin might have had.[24] If anything, Lenin's reputation enjoyed a temporary revival. By the late 1980s, however, this was doubly threatened by a new wave of revisionism in the West running more or less in parallel with revisionism in the Soviet Union.

One of the major themes of this book has been the importance of the most recent historical reassessment. Chapters 3, 4, 5 and especially this chapter have shown how a more detailed study of the masses has reduced the importance of Lenin's leadership in Russia's revolutionary movements. The impact of this on his legacy is strangely mixed. On the one hand, it seems to restate the much more traditional argument that Lenin led to Stalin. It is argued by Robert Service, Edward Acton and others that, having tuned himself into the demands of the peasantry, soldiers and workers during the course of 1917, Lenin switched in 1918 to a policy of repression.[25] The Bolshevik state was created on the premise that power would not be shared with others and the Civil War was as much about suppressing other revolutionaries as it was about preventing counter-revolution. The connection with Stalin is therefore unmistakable.

There is, however, a second perspective. Although it is beyond the scope of this book, Stalin too has been reassessed. Although few would argue that his regime was anything other than ruthless, some historians, such as C. Ward and J. Arch Getty, consider that it was inefficient and that at several stages Stalin came close to losing control of it.[26] This could, of course, be read back to Lenin; the latter did not bequeath a united party, based on tight leadership and operating through effective organs in accordance with an overriding ideology. The Bolsheviks were seriously divided and the regime came close to collapsing from within in 1924. Lenin's real bequest was therefore a ruthless system that none of his successors could make work. For this reason, Lenin was as responsible as Stalin for the eventual collapse of the Soviet Union in 1991.

This remarkable event is the key to revisionist views on Lenin. Until the implosion of the Soviet Union, Lenin was at least credited with making a system that had lasted: it had emerged from the crisis of the purges and invasion by Nazi Germany to become a nuclear superpower. Yet the state that had survived the War eventually died in the peace that followed. This opened a new perspective: instead of guiding Russian history on to a new highway, Lenin had simply shoved it up a cul-de-sac. This is also the point that seems to have been reached by many recent Russian historians, especially Volkogonov.[27] These, of course, have the additional incentive of wanting to see Russia in the twenty-first century rejoin the political mainstream.

SOURCES

THE REPUTATION AND INFLUENCE OF LENIN AFTER 1924

Source A: Extract from G.F. Alexandrov *et al.*, *Joseph Stalin: A Short Biography*, written for the Soviet regime in 1947.

Stalin is the brilliant leader and teacher of the Party, the great strategist of the Socialist Revolution, military commander, and guide of the Soviet state . . . After Lenin, no other leader in the world has been called upon to direct such vast masses of workers and peasant
are his immediate associates, and at the head of the great Bolshevik Party, Stalin guides the destinies of a multi-national Socialist state, a state of workers and

peasants of which there is no precedent in history . . . Stalin is the worthy continuer of the cause of Lenin, or, as it is said in the Party: Stalin is the Lenin of today.

Source B: Extract from *A Short History of the Communist Party of the Soviet Union*, officially endorsed by the Soviet government in 1970. This passage refers to the implementation of Stalin's Five Year Plans before 1940.

More than ever before they [the Soviet people] saw the brilliance of the prevision of the great Lenin, who had drawn up the plan for building socialism in the USSR, and the wisdom of that policy charted by the Communist Party, which firmly and consistently implemented this plan . . .

Having put Lenin's plan into effect and organised and successfully consummated the building of socialism, the Communist Party thus gave the world a model for the revolutionary making of society. The Party had scientifically proved the laws governing this transformation and put these laws to the test of practice.

Source C: Extract from Dmitri Volkogonov, *Lenin: Life and Legacy*, first published in 1994.

Despite the fact that it was doomed to defeat, the Leninist system was extraordinarily viable. This is explained not only by social inertia and the Party's monopoly of power, but also by some of the more attractive features of Leninist 'socialism'. There was its broad base of elementary social security: free education, medicine, holiday pay, accommodation, full employment, a guaranteed minimum wage and much else. The idea of social justice seemed to have found its realization, although, to be sure, all this was accomplished at the cost of the exploitation of the workers and the country's resources.

A closer look reveals that the people's rights and liberties were negligible, and that their lives were led at a level of guaranteed poverty and total dependence on the ideological postulates of the only active political party . . . The life the Soviet people lived for seventy years was not socialism. Without the dictatorship, the Bolsheviks would not have been able to hold on to power and the state they created in 1917. They rejected parliamentary democracy, and Lenin installed his extreme and harsh dictatorship without a second thought . . . We have also seen how easily this destructive approach to the opinions of others escalated into the physical elimination of all those who chose not to fall into line, and how, once absorbed as normal behaviour by the Party, this became an integral and essential feature of the regime in its post-Lenin years.

Source D: Extract from R. Conquest, *Lenin*, published in 1972.

Only believers in historical inevitability would argue that Stalin was inevitable, that he was simply and solely Lenin's heir. But it is at least clear that no very liberal character could have come to lead the Party; that, as a result of the way in which Lenin left the Party organised, it was likely to fall into the hands of the best manipulator of the apparatus . . .

When we consider post-Leninist Russia, we are . . . in the position of judging Lenin (as we are in judging any other historical figure) in the light of hindsight, with knowledge of the results of his actions which he could not possess at the time. Even our hindsight, however, is much cluttered up with myth. There are many widespread notions about the past which have, as it were, entered the public consciousness without adequate verification.

Questions

1. Analyse and explain the differences between Source A and Source B as historical assessments of the continuity between Leninist and Stalinist Russia. (15)
2. Using Sources A to D, explain why the 'legacy of Lenin' has meant different things to different historians. (30)

NOTES

2. OVERVIEW: THE BOLSHEVIK PARTY AND REGIME, 1903–24

1. *A Short History of the Communist Party of the Soviet Union* (Moscow 1970).
2. Max Eastman: *Marx, Lenin, and the Science of Revolution* (London 1926).
3. Christopher Hill: *Lenin and the Russian Revolution* (London 1947).
4. See John Rees: 'In Defence of October', in John Rees, Robert Service, Sam Farber and Robin Blackburn, *In Defence of October: A Debate on the Russian Revolution* (London 1997).
5. Merle Fainsod: *How Russia Is Ruled* (Cambridge, Mass., 1953).
6. Robert Conquest: *Lenin* (London 1972).
7. A. Rabinowitch: *The Bolsheviks Come to Power: The Revolution of 1917 in Petrograd* (New York 1976).

Source A: *A Short History of the Communist Party of the Soviet Union* (Moscow 1970), pp. 128–9.
Source B: Merle Fainsod: *How Russia Is Ruled* (Cambridge, Mass., 1953), pp. 80–6.
Source C: Edward Acton: *Rethinking the Russian Revolution* (London 1990), p. 209.
Source D: Hugh Seton-Watson: *The Decline of Imperial Russia* (London 1952; 1964 edition), pp. 299–300.

3. THE ORIGINS AND GROWTH OF MARXISM IN RUSSIA TO 1905

1. *A Short History of the Communist Party of the Soviet Union* (Moscow 1970), p. 31.
2. *A Short History of the CPSU*, p. 36.

3 Quoted in Stanley W. Page, ed.: *Lenin: Dedicated Marxist or Revolutionary Pragmatist?* (Lexington, Mass., 1970), p. xiii.
4 Max Eastman: *Marx, Lenin, and the Science of Revolution* (London 1926), p. 168.
5 Quoted in Stanley W. Page, ed., p. xiv.
6 James D. White: *Lenin: The Practice and Theory of Revolution* (Basingstoke 2001), p. 28.
7 *A Short History of the CPSU*, pp. 42–3.
8 Rex Wade: *The Russian Revolution, 1917* (Cambridge 2000), p. 11.
9 Orlando Figes: *A People's Tragedy: The Russian Revolution 1891–1924* (London 1996), p. 154.
10 G.D. Obichkin *et al.*: *V.I. Lenin: A Short Biography* (Moscow 1959; 1968 edition), p. 50.
11 Orlando Figes, p. 153.
12 Edmund Wilson: *To the Finland Station* (London 1940; 1968 edition), p. 402.

Source A: Novosti Photo Library.
Source B: V.I. Lenin: *What Is to Be Done*? (1902).
Source C: Sheila Fitzpatrick: *The Russian Revolution* (Oxford 1982; 1994 edition), p. 30.
Source D: Quoted in Michael Lynch: *Reaction and Revolutions: Russia 1881–1924* (London 1992), pp. 41–2.
Source E: Quoted in Orlando Figes: *A People's Tragedy: The Russian Revolution 1891–1924* (London, 1996), p. 153.
Source F: Orlando Figes, p. 153.
Source G: Edmund Wilson: *To the Finland Station* (London 1940; 1968 edition), pp. 400–2.

4. THE BOLSHEVIKS BETWEEN 1903 AND MARCH 1917

1 *A Short History of the Communist Party of the Soviet Union* (Moscow 1970), pp. 62–5.
2 G.D. Obichkin *et al.*: *V.I. Lenin: A Short Biography* (Moscow 1968 edition), p. 52.
3 James D. White, Lenin: *The Practice and Theory of Revolution* (Basingstoke 2001), p. 74.
4 See Christopher Hill: *Lenin and the Russian Revolution* (London 1947), Chapter 5.
5 Quotations from G.D. Obichkin *et al.*, pp. 52–69.
6 Hugh Seton-Watson: *The Decline of Imperial Russia* (London 1952; 1968 edition), pp. 298–9.
7 Anthony Wood: *The Russian Revolution* (Harlow 1982), p. 22.
8 See James D. White, Chapter 3.

9 Quotations from *A Short History of the CPSU*, pp. 70–84.
10 Quotations from *A Short History of the CPSU*, pp. 86–96.
11 James D. White, p. 99
12 Robert Service: 'Lenin', in Edward Acton, Vladimir Iu. Cherniaev and William G. Rosenberg, eds: *Critical Companion to the Russian Revolution 1914–1921* (London 2001), p. 153.
13 Robert Service, p. 153.
Source A: B. Dmytryshyn, ed.: *Imperial Russia: A Source Book* (Hinsdale, Ill., n.d.), pp. 396–7.
Source B: Michael Lynch: *Reaction and Revolution: Russia 1881–1924* (London 1992), p. 48.
Source C: Sheila Fitzpatrick: *The Russian Revolution* (Oxford 1982; 1994 edition), p. 35.
Source D: *A Short History of the Communist Party of the Soviet Union* (Moscow 1970), pp. 94–6.
Source E: David Fry: *Russia: Lenin and Stalin* (London 1966).
Source F: Rex Wade: *The Russian Revolution, 1917* (Cambridge 2000), pp. 25–6.

5. THE BOLSHEVIKS AND THE OCTOBER REVOLUTION

1 Quotations from *A Short History of the Communist Party of the Soviet Union* (Moscow 1970), pp. 113–24.
2 Quotations from G.D. Obichkin *et al.*: *V.I. Lenin: A Short Biography* (Moscow 1968 edition), pp. 141–2.
3 Quoted in Arthur E. Adams: *The Russian Revolution and Bolshevik Victory: Why and How?* (Boston 1960), p. xvi.
4 See Merle Fainsod: *How Russia Is Ruled* (Cambridge, Mass., 1953), pp. 80–6.
5 Edward Acton: *Rethinking the Russian Revolution* (London and New York 1990), especially Chapters 8 and 9.
6 *A Short History of the CPSU*, p. 122.
Source A: V.I. Lenin: *Collected Works* (London 1960), Vol. XXVI, pp. 234–5.
Source B: G. Obichkin *et al.*: *V.I. Lenin: A Short Biography* (Moscow 1959 edition), p. 142.
Source C: Christopher Hill: *Lenin and the Russian Revolution* (London 1947; this edition Harmondsworth 1971), pp. 94–5.
Source D: Robert Wolfson: *Years of Change* (London 1978), p. 329.
Source E: *A Short History of the Communist Party of the Soviet Union* (Moscow 1970), pp. 94–6.
Source F: John Keep: 'Lenin as Tactician', in L. Schapiro and P. Reddaway, eds: *Lenin, the Man, the Theorist, the Leader* (New York 1968), pp. 140–57.

Source G: Alexander Rabinowitch: 'The October Revolution', in Edward Acton, Vladimir Iu. Cheriaev and William G. Rosenberg, eds: *Critical Companion to the Russian Revolution* (London 2001), pp. 82–3.
Source H: Robert Service: 'Lenin: Individual and Politics in the October Revolution', in *Modern History Review*, 1994.

6. THE BOLSHEVIKS AND THE RUSSIAN CIVIL WAR 1918–22

1 See *A Short History of the Communist Party of the Soviet Union* (Moscow 1970), pp. 150–6.
2 See Geoffrey Swain: *The Origins of the Russian Civil War* (London 1996).
3 S. Smith: 'The Socialist-Revolutionaries and the Dilemma of Civil War', in V.N. Brovkin, ed.: *The Bolsheviks in Russian Society* (New Haven and London 1997), p. 84.
4 T. Osipova: 'Peasant Rebellions: Origin, Scope, Dynamics and Consequences', in V.N. Brovkin, ed.: *The Bolsheviks in Russian Society*, p. 173.
5 Quoted in T. Osipova, p. 171.

Source A: Novosti Photo Library.
Source B: Quoted in S.W. Page: *Russia in Revolution* (New Jersey 1965), pp. 152–3.
Source C: Christopher Hill: *Lenin and the Russian Revolution* (London 1947; this edition Harmondsworth 1971), p. 135.
Source D: Quoted in Ronald Kowalski: *The Russian Revolution 1917–1921* (London 1997), Document 8.1, pp. 115–16.
Source E: *A Short History of the Communist Party of the Soviet Union* (Moscow 1970), pp. 162–3.
Source F: Robert Conquest: *Lenin* (London 1972), p. 102.
Source G: Geoffrey Swain: *The Origins of the Russian Civil War* (London 1996), p. 2.

7. THE BOLSHEVIK REGIME, 1918–24

1 Quoted in S.N. Silverman, ed.: *Lenin* (New York 1966), Chapter 2.
2 Quoted in A. Ascher, ed.: *The Mensheviks in the Russian Revolution* (London 1976), Introduction.
3 R. Gregor, ed.: *Resolutions and Decisions of the Communist Party of the Soviet Union*, Vol. 2 (Toronto and Buffalo 1974), Document 2.9.
4 Quoted in G. Leggett: 'Lenin, Terror and the Political Police', in *Survey*, Autumn 1975.

5 Quoted in E.H. Carr: *The Bolshevik Revolution* (London 1950), Vol. 1, Chapter 7.
6 Quoted in A. Erlich: *The Soviet Industrialization Debate 1924–1928* (Cambridge, Mass., 1967), Chapter 1.
7 Quoted in A.G. Mazour, ed.: *Soviet Economic Development: Operation Outstrip, 1921–1965* (Princeton 1967), Chapter 2.
8 *A Short History of the Communist Party of the Soviet Union* (Moscow 1970), p. 130.
9 Quotations from *A Short History of the CPSU*, pp. 165–6.
10 J.L.H. Keep, ed.: *The Debate on Soviet Power: Minutes of the All-Russian Central Executive Committee of Soviets* (Oxford 1979), Introduction.
11 John Rees: 'In Defence of October', in John Rees, Robert Service, Sam Farber and Robin Blackburn, *In Defence of October: A Debate on the Russian Revolution* (London 1997), p. 58.
12 *A Short History of the CPSU*, p. 142.
13 *A Short History of the CPSU*, p. 172.
14 Quoted in D. Lane: *Politics and Society in the USSR* (London 1970), Chapter 3.
15 Dmitri Volkogonov: *Lenin: Life and Legacy* (London 1994), p. 334.
16 Robert Conquest: *Lenin* (London 1972), p. 104.
17 Edward Acton: *Rethinking the Russian Revolution* (London and New York 1990), p. 206.

Source A: Novosti Photo Library.
Source B: *The Essentials of Lenin* (London 1947), Vol. 2, pp. 202–3.
Source C: Quoted in Ronald Kowalski: *The Russian Revolution 1917–1921* (London 1997), Document 7.1, p. 113.
Source D: R.B. Lockhart: *Memoirs of a British Agent* (Harmondsworth 1950), pp. 312–24.
Source E: Martin McCauley: The Russian Revolution and the Soviet State, 1917–1921: *Documents* (London 1975), pp. 184–6.
Source F: *A Short History of the Communist Party of the Soviet Union* (Moscow 1970), pp. 130–5.
Source G: Rex Wade: *The Russian Revolution, 1917* (CUP, Cambridge 2000), pp. 297–8.
Source H: John Rees: 'In Defence of October', in John Rees, Robert Service, Sam Farber and Robin Blackburn, *In Defence of October: A Debate on the Russian Revolution* (London 1997), pp. 29–30.

8. WHICH LENIN?

1. G.D. Obichkin *et al.*: *V.I. Lenin: A Short Biography* (Moscow, 1968 edition), p. 33.
2. G.D. Obichkin *et al.*, p. 43.
3. G.D. Obichkin *et al.*, p. 115.
4. G.D. Obichkin *et al.*, p. 132.
5. G.D. Obichkin *et al.*, p. 29.
6. G.D. Obichkin *et al.*, p. 35.
7. G.D. Obichkin *et al.*, p. 55.
8. G.D. Obichkin *et al.*, p. 141.
9. Merle Fainsod: *How Russia Is Ruled* (Cambridge, Mass., 1953), p. 86.
10. J.L.H. Keep: *The Debate on Soviet Power* (Oxford 1979), p. 173.
11. See R. Pipes: 'The Origins of Bolshevism: The Intellectual Evolution of Young Lenin', in R. Pipes, ed.: *Revolutionary Russia* (London 1968).
12. Adam Ulam: *Lenin and the Bolsheviks* (London 1969), p. 483.
13. See T. Shanin: *Roots of Otherness: Russia's Turn of Century* (London 1986), Vol. 2, pp. 130–1.
14. See A.K. Widman: *The End of the Russian Imperial Army* (Princeton, 1987), Vol. 1, Chapter 7.
15. Rex Wade: *The Russian Revolution, 1917* (Cambridge 2000).
16. Geoffrey Swain: *The Origins of the Russian Civil War* (London 1996).
17. G.D. Obichkin *et al.*, p. 215.
18. Dmitri Volkogonov: *Lenin: Life and Legacy* (London 1994).
19. See Samuel Farber: 'In Defence of Democratic Revolutionary Socialism', in John Rees, Robert Service, Sam Farber and Robin Blackburn, *In Defence of October: A Debate on the Russian Revolution* (London 1997), pp. 101–3.
20. Quoted in G.R. Urban, ed.: *Eurocommunism* (London 1978), pp. 28–9.
21. G. R. Urban, p. 78.
22. Max Eastman: *Marx, Lenin, and the Science of Revolution* (London 1926).
23. Merle Fainsod: *How Russia Is Ruled* (Cambridge, Mass., 1953).
24. Robert Conquest: *The Great Terror* (London 1968).
25. Robert Service: 'Lenin', in Edward Acton, Vladimir Iu. Cherniaev and William G. Rosenberg, eds: *Critical Companion to the Russian Revolution* (London 2001; Edward Acton: *Rethinking the Russian Revolution* (London and New York 1990).
26. C. Ward: *The Stalinist Dictatorship* (London 1998); J. Arch Getty and T. Manning, eds: *Stalinist Terror: New Perspectives* (Cambridge 1993).

27 Dmitri Volkogonov: *Lenin: Life and Legacy* (London 1994).

Source A: G.F. Alexandrov *et al.*: *Joseph Stain: A Short Biography* (Moscow 1947), pp. 198–203.

Source B: *A Short History of the Communist Party of the Soviet Union* (Moscow 1970), pp. 228 and 234.

Source C: Dmitri Volkogonov: *Lenin: Life and Legacy* (London 1994), pp. 483–4.

Source D: Robert Conquest: *Lenin* (London 1972), p. 126.

SELECT BIBLIOGRAPHY

PRIMARY SOURCES

The most comprehensive set of Lenin's writings is in V.I. Lenin: *Collected Works* (London 1960). Edited sources, however, tend to be more accessible for most readers. There are many versions of these. The most helpful collections of sources covering the period are Basil Dmytryshyn, ed.: *Imperial Russia: A Source Book, 1700–1917* (Hinsdale, Ill. 1974); Robert V. Daniels, ed.: *The Russian Revolution* (Englewood Cliffs 1972); F.W. Stacey, ed.: *Lenin and the Russian Revolutions* (London 1968); Martin McCauley, ed.: *The Russian Revolution and the Soviet State* (London 1975); Anthony Wood, ed.: *The Russian Revolution* (Harlow 1982); R. Gregor, ed.: *Resolutions and Decisions of the Communist Party of the Soviet Union*, Vol. 2 (Toronto and Buffalo 1974); and John Daborn, ed.: *Russia: Revolution and Counter-Revolution 1917–1924* (Cambridge 1991). Many new sources are included in what is arguably the best short edition of primary materials: Ronald Kowalski: *The Russian Revolution 1917–1921* (London 1997).

SECONDARY SOURCES

Focus on historiography

This book contains a substantial proportion of historiography. There are several excellent introductions to the range of ideas on Lenin and revolutionary Russia. Three American publications have been available for some time: Arthur E. Adams: *The Russian Revolution and*

Bolshevik Victory: Why and How? (Boston 1960); Robert V. Daniels, ed.: *The Russian Revolution* (Englewood Cliffs 1972); and Stanley W. Page, ed.: *Lenin. Dedicated Marxist or Revolutionary Pragmatist?* (Lexington 1970). The most helpful recent publications are Edward Acton: *Rethinking the Russian Revolution* (London 1990), to which the structure of the historiography in this volume is much indebted, and Edith Rogovin Frankel, Jonathan Frankel and Baruch Knei-Paz: *Revolution in Russia: Reassessments of 1917* (Cambridge 1992). Ronald Kowalski: *The Russian Revolution 1917–1921* (London 1997) contains valuable summaries of different viewpoints in the introductions to the various primary sources.

Background reading on the period

Detailed background reading to the whole period is covered in thousands of different alternatives. Three are worth particular mention: Hugh Seton-Watson: *The Decline of Imperial Russia* (London 1952); Michael T. Florinsky: *Russia: A History and an Interpretation*, Vol. 2 (New York 1953); and an impressive new work: Orlando Figes: *A People's Tragedy: The Russian Revolution 1891–1924* (London 1996). The best known of the earlier works on the Bolshevik period is E.H. Carr: *The Bolshevik Revolution,* 3 vols (London 1950–3) and *The Interregnum* (1954). The most readable survey of the ideological background is still Edmund Wilson: *To the Finland Station* (London 1940).

Soviet and Western non-Soviet viewpoints

A key feature of each interpretative section is an analysis of the official Soviet view of Lenin and the Bolsheviks. The information behind this is taken from two works produced, to the order of the Soviet regime, by committees of historians. These are: N.M. Ponomarev *et al.*: *A Short History of the Communist Party of the Soviet Union* (Moscow 1970); and G.D. Obichkin *et al.*: *V.I. Lenin: A Short Biography* (Moscow 1968 edition).

Two examples of works in Britain reflecting left-wing views, although with some variation between them, are Christopher Hill: *Lenin and the Russian Revolution* (London 1947); and John Rees, Robert Service, Sam Farber and Robin Blackburn, *In Defence of October: A Debate on the Russian Revolution* (London 1997).

Western works have gone through changes of emphasis and approach during the twentieth century, as is outlined in Chapter 8 – some fundamental, others subtle. Among the examples used most frequently in this book are Merle Fainsod: *How Russia Is Ruled* (Cambridge, Mass., 1953); S.N. Silverman, ed.: *Lenin* (New York 1966); Robert Conquest: *Lenin* (London 1972); R. Pipes, ed.: *Revolutionary Russia* (London 1968); L. Schapiro and P. Reddaway, eds: *Lenin, the Man, the Theorist, the Leader* (New York 1968); Adam Ulam: *Lenin and the Bolsheviks* (London 1969); A. Ascher, ed.: *The Mensheviks in the Russian Revolution* (London 1976); Richard Pipes: *The Formation of the Soviet Union: Communism and Nationalism, 1917–1923* (Cambridge, Mass. 1954); J.L.H. Keep, ed.: *The Debate on Soviet Power: Minutes of the All-Russian Central Executive Committee of Soviets* (Oxford 1979); and Robert Service: *The Bolshevik Party in Revolution: A Study in Organizational Change, 1917–1923* (London 1979).

Revisionist works

There has been a huge outpouring of titles on Russia since the launch of *glasnost* by Gorbachev and the collapse of the Soviet Union in 1991. A few have been quoted in this book. These include Sheila Fitzpatrick: *The Russian Revolution* (Oxford 1994 edition) and James D. White: *Lenin: The Practice and Theory of Revolution* (Basingstoke 2001). Particularly impressive are Rex Wade: *The Russian Revolution, 1917* (Cambridge 2000) and Geoffrey Swain: *The Origins of the Russian Civil War* (London 1996). Three composite volumes are very useful. Two, already mentioned, are Edward Acton: *Rethinking the Russian Revolution* (London 1990) and Edith Rogovin Frankel, Jonathan Frankel and Baruch Knei-Paz: *Revolution in Russia: Reassessments of 1917* (Cambridge 1992). The third is Edward Acton, Vladimir Iu. Cherniaev and William G. Rosenberg, eds: *Critical Companion to the Russian Revolution 1914–1921* (London 2001); this has a wide range of contributions, especially from Alexander Rabinowitch ('The October Revolution'), Evan Mawdsley ('The Civil War' and 'The White Armies'), Robert Service ('Lenin' and 'The Bolshevik Party'), Israel Getzler ('Martov'), Michael Melancon ('The Socialist Revolutionary Party'), Alter L. Litvin ('The Cheka'), Orlando Figes ('Peasant Armies' and 'The Peasantry'), Nikolai N. Smirnov ('The Constituent Assembly' and 'The Soviets') and Ronald G. Suny ('Nationality Policies'). Among the most important of recent works from the former Soviet Union is Dmitri Volkogonov: *Lenin: Life and Legacy* (London 1994).

INDEX